Rebuilding Lives after Domestic Violence

by the same author

Supporting Women after Domestic Violence
Loss, Trauma and Recovery
Hilary Abrahams
Foreword by Cathy Humphreys
ISBN 978 1 84310 431 5

Making an Impact – Children and Domestic Violence
A Reader
Second Edition
Marianne Hester, Chris Pearson and Nicola Harwin with Hilary Abrahams
ISBN 978 1 84310 157 4

of related interest

Counselling Survivors of Domestic Abuse
Christiane Sanderson
ISBN 978 1 84310 606 7

Violence Against Women in South Asian Communities
Issues for Policy and Practice
Edited by Ravi K. Thiara and Aisha K. Gill
Foreword by Professor Liz Kelly CBE
ISBN 978 1 84310 670 8

Talking About Domestic Abuse
A Photo Activity Workbook to Develop Communication
between Mothers and Young People
Cathy Humphreys, Ravi K. Thiara, Agnes Skamballis and Audrey Mullender
ISBN 978 1 84310 423 0

Talking to My Mum
A Picture Workbook for Workers, Mothers and Children Affected by
Domestic Abuse
Cathy Humphreys, Ravi K. Thiara, Agnes Skamballis and Audrey Mullender
ISBN 978 1 84310 422 3

Mothering Through Domestic Violence
Lorraine Radford and Marianne Hester
ISBN 978 1 84310 473 5

Domestic Violence and Child Protection
Directions for Good Practice
Edited by Cathy Humphreys and Nicky Stanley
ISBN 978 1 84310 276 2

Rebuilding Lives after Domestic Violence

Understanding Long-Term Outcomes

Hilary Abrahams

Foreword by Jenni Murray OBE

Jessica Kingsley Publishers
London and Philadelphia

First published in 2010
by Jessica Kingsley Publishers
116 Pentonville Road
London N1 9JB, UK
and
400 Market Street, Suite 400
Philadelphia, PA 19106, USA

www.jkp.com

Library of Congress Cataloging in Publication Data
Abrahams, Hilary, 1941-
    Rebuilding lives after domestic violence : understanding long-term
outcomes / Hilary Abrahams ; foreword by Jenni Murray.
        p. cm.
    Includes bibliographical references and index.
    ISBN 978-1-84310-961-7 (alk. paper)
    1. Abused wives. 2. Marital violence--Psychological aspects. 3. Abused
wives--Rehabilitation. 4. Children of abused wives--Rehabilitation. 5. Social
networks. I. Title.
    HV6626.A158 2007
    362.82'92--dc22
                        2009048409

British Library Cataloguing in Publication Data
A CIP catalogue record for this book is available from the British Library

ISBN 978 1 84310 961 7

Printed and bound in Great Britain by
MPG Books Group

*For the twelve women who told their
stories in order to help others, with respect and
admiration for their courage and honesty*

Acknowledgements

This study was made possible through the interest, involvement and support of many women. My thanks go to:

The residents and former residents of refuges and safe houses in York, Birmingham, Penzance, Derby, Devizes and Alton who took part in this research and who wanted to share their experiences and thoughts in order to create a better understanding of their issues and support needs and to help other women.

The workers, volunteers and managers at the refuges who participated so enthusiastically and took time out of their busy days in order to work with me.

All the members of Women's Aid who helped to shape this research with their ideas, comments and feedback.

My friends and colleagues who provided support, shared their expertise and offered helpful comments: Ellen, Emma, Hilary, Jackie, Jane, Jo and Rebecca.

And finally to Ian, for his unfailing support and encouragement over many years, without which none of this would have been possible.

The original research was a collaborative project between the Violence against Women Research Group, School for Policy Studies, University of Bristol, and the Women's Aid Federation of England. It was supported by a grant from the Economic and Social Research Council.

The evaluation of supported housing was commissioned and funded by the Office of the Deputy Prime Minister, UK (now the Department for Communities and Local Government).

The longitudinal study was supported by funding from The British Academy (grant number SG-41644).

Contents

Foreword

I can think of nothing more terrifying than finding that the home you expected would be a place of comfort and refuge has become the centre of a life where physical violence and complete psychological control dominate every move you make. Personally, I have been extremely fortunate. My grandfather and father were the kindest and gentlest of men. My partner and two adult sons show me nothing but love and respect. But I know that there are many thousands of women who have no life of their own because the men they believed they could love and trust won't let them.

We hear very little that is hopeful on the subject of domestic violence. The statistics are horrific: two women every week are killed by a partner or former partner. Children are caught up in a cycle of abuse. Despite the best efforts of charities such as Refuge and Women's Aid, there is still a woeful lack of accommodation for women and children who try to escape. And so often we hear that old chestnut trotted out, 'Well, why didn't she just get out?'

This book gives women the opportunity to explain why they were powerless to leave; to describe how having no money, nowhere to go and no confidence in your ability to stand on your own two feet and protect yourself and your children makes the mere prospect of leaving seem impossible.

Most importantly, we hear from women who have found the courage to walk away and find a new life where violence and dominance play no part. It is a testament to the bravery and resourcefulness of women who have suffered unimaginable humiliation and cruelty at the hands of a man they thought would love them. It is full of hope.

by Jenni Murray OBE

Introduction

Every year, thousands of women take the difficult decision to leave an abusive relationship. Many stay for a time in refuges, or safe houses, where they and their children can receive practical and emotional support. Sometimes they will return to their abuser, but later gain the strength to leave again. Eventually, if they stay away, they will be able to start a new life in the wider community, and often support from the refuge will continue while they settle in. But what happens to these women and their children five, six, seven, even eight years down the line? What are the pressures and difficulties they face in their new lives? Where do they draw strength and support from? And how do they feel about themselves, the possibility of new relationships and the future for themselves and their children?

In this book, women whom I first met during their stay in a refuge talk openly and honestly about themselves: the challenges and barriers they face and their emotional vulnerability. Not all could tell success stories; there were achievements to celebrate, but also, for some, continuing losses, and, for most of them, the shadows of fear and anxiety to contend with. They talked to me also about the support they had received: what had been most useful and what other assistance would have helped. From these conversations and from the workers in this field, I have been able to identify the factors that appear to assist or hinder the successful transition to independent living and key areas where enhanced service provision could be of value in helping social integration.

This is the first study since the late 1970s to follow women from the refuge into their new lives, and the only one to cover such an extended period. Because all of the women were interviewed while in a refuge, followed, for the majority, by a further interview six months on and then again for this research, it shows clearly the process of change in their lives and the extent to which problems remained. It is unique in offering contemporary factual evidence on the long-term effects of domestic violence and abuse and of women's needs in areas such as housing, health and employment. Service provision to date has largely, and understandably, focused on much-needed refuge accommodation and the immediate period after rehousing. Although refuges have been, and are, vitally important in providing front-line support for women leaving an abusive relationship, we need to move beyond this to consider how best to enable women to integrate fully into their new communities and contribute their skills to society. By exploring the longer-term needs of families, this study adds a new dimension to service provision and offers valuable insights into this process for both policy makers and service providers. It offers information and understandings that can facilitate the provision of appropriate, targeted and cost-effective services; in particular, the low-level support, over an extended period, which may reduce the need for higher-level (and more expensive) interventions at a later date. On a practical level, the work will be of use not only to refuge groups providing resettlement, outreach or floating support, but also to a wide range of support services in the community and to professional and voluntary agencies, including health professionals, housing officers and counsellors, who come into contact with these women.

About the project

This research built on two previous studies looking at the practical and emotional support needs of women who had experienced domestic violence, immediately after leaving an abusive relationship, during their stay in a refuge or safe house, and shortly after rehousing.[1] Although both of these projects produced valuable information, I felt that some indication of longer-term outcomes could provide important information on women's needs after leaving the refuge, help to identify any gaps in service provision and assist the development of services structured to meet the long-term needs of women and their families. Many of those who talked to me during these studies had said they would welcome the opportunity to meet up again after a few years, to talk about how they were getting on. All of the refuges involved in the earlier projects saw the value to them of gaining this information and were enthusiastic about helping with the research. Together, and supported by a grant from The British Academy, we established that safe contact could be made with 22 women whose whereabouts were known (just over half of those in the original groups) and twelve of them responded positively (54.5%). Three of these women came from the first study and nine from the more recent interviews; in addition, I received firm information, either from workers or other women, on the longer-term outcomes for a further eleven women. Five of these were from the group who were not directly contactable, either because they had withheld their addresses or because contact was considered unsafe, and six from those who had chosen not to respond. There was also a wide range of anecdotal evidence on outcomes for other women, but no firm information to validate these. Most of the women who responded had been out of the original abusive relationship for more than five years; two had made the break over seven years ago. Although they were very different from each other in age, family make-up, background and geographical location, there was remarkable consistency from all of them as to what was important, where problems arose for them and where they saw gaps in service provision. Their comments, thoughts and opinions are consistent with other research on short- to medium-term outcomes[2] and validate previous anecdotal evidence on the long-term effects of domestic violence and abuse. More information about the research participants, the ethical and safety considerations involved and the methodology can be found in Appendix 1.

About the book

Chapter 1 looks at the way the women saw themselves as they prepared to leave the refuge: their mental and physical readiness to start their new lives, the extent of their coping abilities, and their hopes and expectations for the future. It also examines the emotional 'baggage' they carried with them: the multiple losses, the corrosive effects of domestic violence and abuse on their confidence and self-respect, and the consequential reluctance to risk placing trust in another human being. For women, there is immense significance to the concept of 'home', and Chapter 2 explores the experience of being rehoused, the challenges of starting from scratch, and how the process of turning a house into a home began a similar transformatory process within the women themselves.

The next two chapters deal with the growth of networks and relationships. Chapter 3 examines the nature and extent of support systems, the barriers to obtaining help and the role of resettlement workers, whereas Chapter 4 broadens this discussion to look at the need to build relationships that would sustain them in their daily lives – first with friends and the community around them – and then to examine the tension between the desire for another intimate relationship and the memory of past love and trust betrayed.

Often, women who experience domestic violence are denied any opportunity to organise or manage any aspect of their daily lives. Chapter 5 considers the steep learning curve that was involved for many of them in learning to live independently, the need to provide leisure opportunities for themselves and their children, and the options available in terms of work, training and further education. Physical and mental health are explored in Chapter 6, including the reduced use of substances such as drugs, alcohol and tobacco, the extent to which counselling services had been helpful, and the underlying fear and anxiety caused by the shadowy presence of the abuser. All of the women were mothers, and Chapter 7 looks at their concerns and hopes for their children, the problems which had arisen, and the difficulties the women had experienced in accessing appropriate and timely help.

Stepping back from discussion of the day-to-day situation, in Chapter 8, the women look at the changes that have taken place in their lives over the preceding years: the growth of their inner strength and determination, and the rediscovery of their own identity and personal values. The factors that appear to have contributed to these changes and those that have facilitated a successful transition to independent living are examined, and the women offer their thoughts on the controversial topic of women for women services. In contrast with their earlier interviews, most of the women now felt they had a future, and Chapter 9 looks forward to their longer-term aims and asks if their hopes and expectations on leaving the refuge (outlined in Chapter 1) had been realised. It also reports on the need the women felt to 'give something back' and the extent to which they were fulfilling this desire by reaching out to help others who were struggling with problems in their lives. And, finally, at the end of our last interview, I asked the women what message they would like to send to other women who might be enduring domestic violence and abuse. Their messages range from practical advice on obtaining evidence, dealing with the perpetrator and the mechanics of leaving, to words of hope and encouragement about the new life they have found. They are deeply moving and offer positive and inspirational material to the reader.

Making the choice to respond

There are a number of possible reasons why ten of the women whom I contacted chose not to respond: they may have felt that they had not lived up to the hopes and expectations expressed in previous interviews and seen this as a 'failure'; they may have decided to close the door on the past and did not wish to be reminded of it; or they might have been in a new relationship and felt that talking to me might jeopardise this.

Yet twelve women, who, on the surface, seemed no different from the other women I had met and who might well have initially had similar thoughts, had chosen to respond. I wondered what were the reasons that had influenced them. What was it that had made them choose to contact me? One of the key factors, they felt, was that I had met them before and built up trust that I would listen and bear accurate witness to their stories. They also appreciated having a space in their lives to reflect on their progress and think about where they were going. Most wanted to show me how far they had come: the effort and ingenuity that had gone into the creation of a real home for themselves and their children, education, holidays, perhaps a job and, for some, a new and non-violent partner. But not all were success stories, and the women also wanted to discuss their struggles on a personal level and the difficulties they had faced and were still facing.

But the major factor for all of them was the intense desire for their knowledge to reach a wider audience. They wanted to share their experiences so that other women who might be experiencing domestic violence and abuse could learn from their journeys: to understand the challenges, but also all that they had gained from leaving.[3] And they wanted to tell women that it was possible to come through it. As Sally[4] put it, 'every time I seen you, my life's been getting better. I just wanted to say to others that it does get better. Tell people you *can* pick up your life again.'

They also felt it was important to raise awareness of abuse in general. Lindy commented that 'Society needs to understand'. By taking part, they hoped that their experiences could make a positive impact on others. Gemma saw this clearly:

> I will not wreck this experience. I have to make something good out of it, otherwise I suffered for no reason…and that… that's not acceptable to me. I've got scars on my face, you know, I lost every…so much and it's…yeah, I can't waste the experience, I do have to do something with it. And right now I'm not able to, but you can. So I have to share anything that could be put to use for other people.

It is these voices that resonate through the rest of this book. Their stories, from the time I first met them in the refuge to our last meeting, show how their lives have changed over the years and provide an insight into the lengthy and difficult process of rebuilding lives after the experience of domestic violence and abuse.

Notes

1. The first study was carried out for the Women's Aid Federation of England and has now been published (Abrahams 2007). The second study formed part of a much larger project examining the housing and support needs of vulnerable groups, carried out on behalf of the Office of the Deputy Prime Minister (now the Department for Communities and Local Government). As well as women who had experienced domestic violence and abuse, it included young people leaving care, ex-offenders, teenage parents, and individuals with drug, alcohol or mental health problems. The relevant reports are now available on the internet (Supporting People 2007).

2. Hoff 1990; Humphreys and Thiara 2002; Kirkwood 1993.

3. This reason for participating was also identified by Hoff (1990), Humphreys and Thiara (2002) and the Women's Budget Group (2008).

4. The names of women, children and workers have been changed throughout to preserve anonymity and confidentiality, and no reference is made to the locality they came from or the area where they have now settled.

Chapter 1

A New Journey – With Old Baggage

Starting on a different pathway in our lives is always exciting and a little frightening. Whether it is a comparatively small step, such as signing up to learn a new skill, or a major change – starting a new job, moving to a new home, or even a new country – we have expectations about what it will be like, hopes about how we would like things to turn out and speculations as to what it might lead to. But there will also be fears about what lies ahead and whether we will be able to make a success of it. Some of these feelings may be shaped by past memories of success or failure, others by the positive or negative attitudes of those around us, by what we have read or people we meet who have done the same thing.

All these factors will influence the way we approach our new venture and play a part in its long-term outcomes. Women who have left an abusive relationship and are on the point of being rehoused in a new community are no different in this respect; their hopes centre on a new life free from violence and their fears are shaped by their experience of abuse and their need for safety and security. For the women who talked to me, moving back into the wider community created fears that had to be faced, but also revealed their determination to make a success of this new venture. In this chapter, they explore these issues, talk about their hopes and expectations as they waited to be rehoused and discuss the effect that domestic violence and abuse had had on their mental and emotional well-being.

Hopes and expectations

When I first met these women, between five and eight years previously, their hopes and expectations for the future were, in the main, direct and simple. They wanted a new home, a new beginning:

> All I want is a fresh start and a new life where nobody knows me. (Leanne)

> It is a new start for me. (Sally)

> To turn my life around. (Molly)

> A nice home. (Maddy)

Some of them went beyond these basic needs to express their wider hopes for themselves and their children. Sylvia wanted to see her children 'safe, secure and happy'. And for herself? 'Peace. I'm not going to be afraid any more of who comes to the front door.' Keira was also beginning to see a bigger picture – 'to get my life back on track, set up home, make sure the children are safe and secure and feel happy'. And for others, there was also a yearning for there to be something more to their lives and for personal success and achievement:

> To get a job with respect and a long-term future. (Jeannie)

> Get my life back on track, get my self-confidence back. I want a good life. I want to just get out there and get on with things. (Charmian)

> I want to do so much, because I've never been allowed to. …And…I know I'll be good at it, I know I will, because I've always wanted to do things. (Liz)

Two women had been so traumatised by their experiences of abuse that, at that stage of their lives, they were unable to formulate any concept of a future. Gemma felt dazed and helpless: 'I'm so bleeding from all the nastiness he put me through. One day at a time. I can't plan that far.' Briony said, 'I haven't got a clue. Just take one day at a time. All you can do.'

It was not always those who might have been seen as most vulnerable who lacked a vision of their future. I met Lindy when she had been in the refuge for just three days, discharged from hospital after taking an overdose as a consequence of the emotional abuse she had suffered. Her hands were visibly shaking as she lit cigarette after cigarette while she talked. But she had a clear picture of what she wanted in her future:

> I'm hoping I'm going to have my own home, I'm going to be working, providing for my children. I want to be back to my normal weight that I usually am. I was nine stone when I met my husband. I want him crawling on his bent knees to come back to me and I'm hoping

I'm going to be strong enough to…excuse my language…go…(*makes gesture*) to him. That's what I would love. I hope I'm going to be strong enough to say 'Too late'.

Effects of domestic violence and abuse

In listening carefully to the early hopes and dreams about their new lives, there are clear indications of the impact that domestic violence and abuse had had on these women. They wanted safety and security, to live without fear, to be free to act for themselves, and to be treated with respect and valued – the converse of the situations they had endured previously. Other indications of the effects of abuse became apparent as they talked: a total lack of confidence, difficulty in trusting either themselves or others, and major problems with making decisions. To understand this 'emotional baggage' and the influence this would have on their ability to rebuild their lives, we need to look at the destructive way in which abuse impacts on every aspect of the lives of those who experience it.

Domestic violence and abuse in England and Wales has been defined officially as:

> Any incident of threatening behaviour, violence or abuse (psychological, physical, sexual, financial or emotional) between adults who are, or have been, intimate partners or family members, regardless of gender or sexuality. This includes issues of concern to black and minority ethnic (BME) communities such as so-called 'honour based violence', female genital mutilation (FGM) and forced marriage. (Home Office 2009)

The Scottish Executive (2009) have adopted a more nuanced definition (as have many local authorities), accepting that, although some men are abused by women and there can be violence within same-sex relationships, domestic violence is most commonly perpetrated by men against women and cuts across class, age, religion and ethnic group. They point out the degrading and humiliating aspects of sexual abuse, and their definition also brings into greater prominence the issue of mental and emotional abuse, which can include threats, verbal and racial abuse, withholding money and various forms of controlling behaviour, such as isolation from friends and family. It was this emotional abuse that had been a major issue for the women who talked to me; horrific though some of the physical and sexual violence inflicted on many of them had been, it was the direct and indirect effects of abuse on their mental and emotional well-being that had scarred them most deeply. It had removed any sense of safety and security, destroyed their belief in themselves and their abilities, damaged their links to the community around them and their access to sources of support. Yet, paradoxically, this type of abuse was the hardest to talk about and for others to understand, because of its almost invisible nature. As Lindy said, 'If it was a broken bone, you'd understand it, because you could see it.'

For most of the women, the growth of the abusive behaviour had been a slow progression, as what had seemed like loving care and concern for them gradually constricted and controlled every aspect of their lives and thoughts. They spoke of the way the world appeared to be 'closing in' on them, as their partner began to control their interaction with friends and family. Sylvia described how this process had slowly affected her and how fear grew:

> And I think as the violence and everything progressed I kind of…my world closed in and closed in and closed in. And then, unfortunately, outside of the children, he was my total centre and yet he was the aggressor. So that's where that kind of became where you didn't speak, you didn't say. And all these things that people say when they see it on TV – 'What did that bloomin' stupid woman put up with that for?' you know. But they don't realise how our world…it takes a long time, it's over years, you know. They'll say something about one friend, make that friend feel uncomfortable and they'll drop off and drop off and drop off. And suddenly this centre closes down and suddenly the person who's the worst is the only person you have left. So you start living in this kind of walking on egg shells scenario, you know, of just hoping that every day is going to be okay and don't say anything, don't tell anybody. It is that shrinking world that is so slow a process.

This shrinking world included giving up jobs or having to refuse a promotion, perhaps because of a flat refusal to help with childcare, or sometimes because jealous behaviour in the home or at the workplace, became too much to handle. Nor were family and friends the only casualties: shopping trips and chats across the garden fence became equally suspect, leaving women dependent on their abuser for any form of interaction and daily conversation. This was inevitably negative and belittling, directive of their behaviour and critical of their appearance, abilities and intelligence. Gemma explained a little of what she had experienced:

> You know, he'd have a mard if I wouldn't spend time with him and he'd say I should clean, when I'd clean. And…Oh God, the way I looked and if somebody would text me in a friendly way that was male, I was shagging them. And if I had a female friend, I must be shagging them. So I became very much his property, actually.

Controlled like this and under a constant stream of criticism, the women began to lose their sense of personal integrity, of being a person in their own right, with their own ideas and ideals. They lost confidence and respect for themselves as people who were worthy of existing. Some, like Lindy, had attempted suicide in this belief, or as the only way to end the pain; more had considered it. This sense of complete and utter worthlessness, lack of confidence and of belief in themselves was the feeling that came across most strongly in the first interviews. Woman after woman spoke of the way confidence had drained away through the emotional abuse they had experienced. Jeannie's abusive partner did not live permanently with her, but she had suffered in the same way:

> I was that low. I felt like nothing. I couldn't even hold my head up on the street. I just felt like…I just felt like nothing, and then having someone telling you constantly you're nothing – you've got two different fathers for your kids, no one's ever going to want you. You're nothing, you've got nothing. You know, just destroying you. I mean what he did to me physically I can't even remember.

In this way, the abuser's negative views about them became internalised and reflected in their own thoughts and feelings about themselves. The shame and guilt that the women felt about their situation meant that, like Sylvia, most of them told no one about what was happening to them. Nor were they sure that anything those outside the relationship could say or do would assist; indeed, it might make things significantly worse, provoking further physical and/or emotional violence towards them, their children or the person who had intervened. Consequently, they became increasingly unsure about whom they could trust and turn to, since they were being abused by someone whom they had trusted and who claimed to love them. They no longer believed in themselves and were uncertain as to how others would react to them, especially since the abuser often seemed, to those outside the relationship, to be a respected individual with good social skills and a confident approach to life. These fears made them very wary of approaching or placing trust in any individual or organisation. Lindy, like the majority of the women who spoke to me, was clear about how abuse had destroyed any sense of trust in herself or others: 'I don't trust people any more. I've been hurt so many times.' This growing fear of approaching others, together with isolation from friends, family and other social contacts, meant that there were fewer contacts that might offer a different perspective on events, or challenge women's views of themselves.

Once the initial incident of abuse, whether physical, sexual or emotional, had taken place, fear and anxiety formed an undercurrent to their existence and, as the abuse continued, daily life became increasingly unpredictable and frightening; although they were unable to predict *when* a further incident would take place, or exactly *what* would happen, they were always waiting for *something* to happen, so that there was no sense of physical and mental safety in their lives. And since anything they, or their children, did had the potential to be seen as 'wrong' by their abuser, there was no framework for daily life, no 'reference points' except the inevitability of abuse at some point. Sally simply said, 'I was so frightened of…everything.'

All of these separate elements of abuse – isolation, fear, loss of self-worth and controlling behaviour – fed on and reinforced each other, so that women felt trapped in a downward spiral of despair. But other feelings were also in evidence, since their abuser was still often capable of showing loving and gentle behaviour towards them, and many of the women retained feelings of love and loyalty towards him or her. Additionally, for the majority of the women, their abuser was also the father of some or all of their children, giving a further dimension to their relationship. These mixed, ambivalent and painful feelings left the women confused and uncertain as to what was happening, yet they did not see themselves as totally helpless or passive within the relationship; within the constraints imposed on them, they were doing their best to care for themselves and their children. Knowing, better than anyone else, what the level of risk to themselves and their children was likely to be at any one time, they monitored their behaviour and that of their children ('walking on eggshells', as Sylvia described it),[1] acted to defuse tensions, and tried to please and satisfy their abuser. Where it was possible to do so without triggering further abusive behaviour, they tried to maintain links with others and evolved a wide variety of strategies to cope with the situation.[2] And although there were times when they almost gave up the struggle to survive, somehow they found the strength to keep going.

Making sense of the effects of abuse

In seeking to understand the way in which domestic violence and abuse had undermined every aspect of these women's lives and also their determination to survive and to reach out to others, it can be helpful to consider Maslow's[3] ideas on human needs. He argued that, as well as their basic physiological needs for survival (food, water, shelter and clothing), individuals have levels of personal and emotional needs that they actively want to satisfy. Once the basics necessary for existence were at least partially met, they would put energy and effort into looking for some measure of safety and freedom from fear. As this need began to be satisfied, they then wanted to feel a sense of belonging, of being part of a community, and to connect and be accepted by those around them. If this connection to others could be established, individuals then looked to experience feelings of self-esteem, confidence and self-respect and finally sought to develop their own abilities and capabilities, in whatever direction these might lie. What holds people back from meeting their needs, in Maslow's view, are the social and economic disadvantages they face, and the memory of past experiences that have damaged or blocked their capacity to act. These ideas are often shown as a pyramid of five building blocks.

The stories of these women show clearly how domestic violence and abuse had demolished this structure with the loss of their personal identity, the destruction of their confidence and self-esteem, isolation from potential support systems, and the growth of fear and uncertainty. For some, even access to the basic needs for survival had been controlled and denied, and, for all of them, their capacity to act had been severely restricted by their

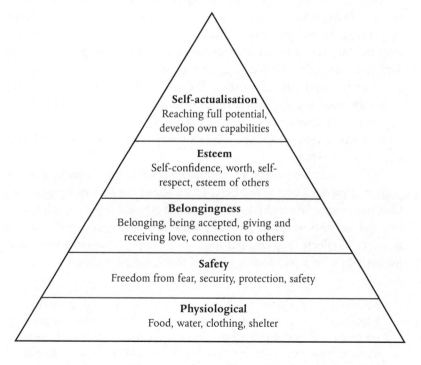

Figure 1.1 Maslow's Hierarchy of Human Need (1987, first published 1954)

abusers. Yet they still had a determination to survive, to protect themselves and their children, to reach out to others, and to take whatever positive action seemed possible to move forward in their lives.

The process of leaving

It can be hard, both for the general public and for those who have professional contacts with women who experience domestic violence and abuse, to understand why they don't 'just leave'. Complex and conflicting issues and emotions, however, make taking the decision to leave immensely difficult. As the two previous sections have shown, women could still feel love, as well as fear and hatred, towards their abuser, and their confidence and power of independent action had become seriously eroded by the abuse. In leaving, they would have to uproot themselves from their homes, lose contact with any remaining social network and any financial support from their partner. And leaving would also mean taking a frightening leap into the unknown. Where would they go? How would they manage? And who would be there for them?

Nor is leaving necessarily the safest course of action. Homicide statistics in England and Wales show that the majority of women are killed by partners, former partners, or lovers,[4] and at the point of departure, or after leaving, is commonly considered to be the time of greatest danger. And violence short of killing does not necessarily stop after leaving. For a substantial minority of women, abuse in some form continues long after they have left the relationship: Briony and Molly had been living independently after leaving a relationship, but were still suffering physical and emotional violence to the extent that they needed to leave their homes and go into a refuge.

The women who talked to me identified three main reasons that had pushed them into taking the decision to leave: the realisation that their lives and those of their children were in immediate danger, a sudden surge of anger, or the final realisation that things were never going to change and that all the efforts they had put into making the relationship work were useless. No sooner had Maddy reached this conclusion than she acted:

> Well, I'll tell you what happened. I went to work and… He was being a bit…funny, at the time. So I went to work. Well, they'd see'd me with a few bruises – I've been to work nearly three years and they've see'd me black and blue and they've said 'It's about time you did summat about it.' I wouldn't take no notice. So, everyone said it was up to me. So I made my mind up on that particular day. So I went to work, did

me work, came…and I think they'd got an inkling that I weren't coming back. But it wasn't for them to say. So I went home, I got the kids. He was fast asleep. I'd got money upstairs from work. I just took me bag, the kids, no clothes nor anything. I walked. I had a mobile phone and I rang my oldest son and I said, 'I've walked out. I'm going.'

Others, like Charmian, took longer to separate out their feelings and were able to plan their exit strategy:

I mean I had to be strong, I was determined. I planned it, like, two maybe three months, getting out of here. 'I'm getting out of here.' That's all I kept saying to myself. 'I hate him.' …I loved him but I hated him. I shoved the love to one side and kept thinking to myself, 'I hate him, I hate him, I'm getting out of here now.' You know, I never ever thought I'd have the strength to get out. But I mean he nearly left me for dead every day. But um… But I got out while he was still in the house, and I couldn't believe I did it. You know I didn't even look round. I just…(*laughs*) Andrew in't pushchair, grabbed all his wages and I just shot through it. Left him without a penny!

A number of the women had left before and stayed with friends or family, before returning in a further attempt to make the relationship work. Two of them had also been in refuges before, but told me that, in their last decision to leave, there had been a feeling that the time had been right for a permanent exit. Both women felt that they had gained in confidence at each visit and that they would not be returning. Liz had been through this process on a number of occasions: 'This is the fifth time. Fifth. And last.' Keira, whose final decision to leave had been an impulse of anger, following an extreme incident of physical violence, reflected that she had been gradually changing with each refuge visit:

It was a long time. It wasn't the first refuge I'd been in, it was probably the fourth. But I knew, this time, I was ready to move on and make a life of my own. Several years ago, again with the younger children, I'd moved into a refuge and at that time I wasn't ready to move on. I think I knew that when I went. But this time… You have to be ready yourself, don't you? I'd been in this violent relationship for 30 years. No one can tell you. You have to be ready in your own thoughts to do it. I think what it was, because I had become a different person.

Taking the decision to leave meant the loss of a relationship in which they had invested all their hopes, time and energy, and that had been the total focus of their lives for many years. It meant the loss of their homes, most of their material possessions, sometimes older children and pets who had had to be left behind, and exchanging familiar surroundings for an alien environment. Not surprisingly, when they arrived at the refuge, they were, as they told me, 'shell-shocked' – dazed and numb from their experiences and from the sheer effort of leaving. Several recognised that the impact of their multiple losses was similar to the emotions experienced after bereavement,[5] and that, as Briony commented, they had to deal with 'all the pain and grief of leaving', before beginning to adjust to what had happened, make sense of their experiences and move on. The refuge offered a safe space for this reconstruction to begin.

As explored more fully in Chapter 8, it was this feeling of mental and physical safety that the women recalled as having been most important to them at that time. But they also valued being a member of a community that understood and accepted them, gave them social contact and practical and emotional support. Exactly as Maslow (Figure 1.1, page 23) suggested, these factors created the conditions that began to restore their confidence and self-esteem. The allocation of a property, however, marked the beginning of a further major change in their lives: they began to realise, with some apprehension, that they would be leaving this behind and would be, once more, fully responsible for their survival. At the same time, however, there was excitement at the prospect of having a new home and a fresh start.

An emotional roller coaster

For some women, the sheer euphoria of getting a house was momentarily overwhelming. After moving between refuges with her two young sons for nearly two years, Jeannie couldn't believe what had happened:

> Oh God! I thought it was absolutely beautiful, I couldn't believe it. I was screaming and the landlord was looking at me like I was mad. My key worker, Viv, she was here and she said, 'Oh', she said that…she goes, 'She's just really, really, happy, just sort of finally.' Because 19 months I was in refuges. And, like, as soon as I came in…as soon as I looked outside I thought, 'Wow!' When I looked inside I thought, 'My God'…and I was just screaming and jumping up and down. And then my mobile went, it was my friend and I was like 'I've got somewhere!' and I was screaming down the phone. You know.

Running in parallel with this excitement were the underlying fears that were directly related to their past experience: fears about being alone, of making their own decisions, of their whereabouts becoming known to the perpetrator. Wrestling with these two conflicting strands of emotions created what Lindy described as 'a roller-coaster ride':

> Why am I feeling like this? 'Cos I think when we got the housing…we got told we've got a house, and here's me thinking…first of all I was like 'Yes', and then I went 'Oh…' and it was back on the roller coaster again. Emotions have sort of gone up down, up down, and then we had this…like, got told we'd got a house, and then we were back up on this roller coaster…oh my God it's like…and like Lydia [worker] was there, 'Come on, you'll be all right, this is normal', you know. So that side of it, she's sort of confirmed this is a normal procedure to go through, you will…you'll probably get in your new house and sob your heart out, but…

These emotional ups and downs were something they had experienced when they first came to the refuge,[6] and it was confusing and frightening to find a similar pattern surfacing, just when they felt they should be happy.

The thought of being alone with just their children was usually one of the earliest concerns about leaving that they voiced in our talks. Yes, they would, they hoped, be living free from continuing violence, but there would also not be any other adult to share the responsibilities of daily life. Within the refuge, there had been a supportive community, with other women who had experienced domestic violence and abuse. Not only had this given them a social network to replace the isolation caused by the abuse, but it also ensured that there were always other women to turn to if they were scared by unusual noises in the night or by an unexpected knock on the door. Now, there would be no one else there.

Similar fears were expressed about the prospect of managing and making decisions alone. Women who had been told when and how to clean their houses, whose shopping had been strictly controlled, and who had never been allowed to manage their own money or make decisions on behalf of the family, faced an immense learning curve. Sometimes, they had been so regulated that they had no idea how organisations worked, or where to apply for what they needed, but for all of them, the prospect of making decisions on their own behalf was exhilarating, though at the same time intimidating. The denigration, control and criticism they had suffered had not only destroyed their trust in others; it had caused them to lose confidence and trust in themselves and their ability to make judgements, weigh up possibilities and make the right decision. Their lack of self-worth also affected how they felt about taking charge in this way. Liz struggled to explain how she felt:

> Because, I suppose, it is hard to, like, think for yourself and, like, think, well… Because you feel you're low…you just feel like nothing and you've got to start from scratch and…I don't know, it's dead hard to explain.

Moving from a controlling relationship to the refuge had provided a halfway house, where there was a framework of house rules, but where women were encouraged to make decisions for themselves, with support from workers and other residents. Now, although there might be further support available from outreach services and other agencies, they would have to take on the responsibility of making choices and decisions for themselves and their children, choices that would affect their lives in both the short and longer term. When I talked to Briony, soon after she had moved to her new home, she confirmed how difficult this was proving to be: 'It is hard, because you lose the security of the place where you're at. It is hard to adjust again.'

The security she spoke of was not simply the security of a supportive community, with advice and guidance readily available, but the physical and mental security of knowing that the abuser could not gain access to the refuge. This was the most pervasive fear for the majority of the women: of being traced by their former partners and what action they, or their families, might take once the women had left the safety of the refuge. This fear, discussed further in Chapter 5, was to cast a shadow over their lives for many years to come, even when they had moved long distances and perhaps assumed new identities.

These very real fears about their new lives and their ability to cope need to be set against the background of what these women had already achieved. They had survived physical, emotional and sexual violence and abuse. They had been tenacious and skilful in their efforts to survive and protect themselves and their children. They had taken the immense step of leaving and they were determined to make out in their new environment, as their hopes and dreams of the future showed. And there was also a strong element of wanting to prove that their abuser was wrong about them and their abilities. 'I want to prove,' Charmian said, 'that I wasn't such a useless piece of weight like he always said I was.' In tracing the destructive effects of domestic violence and abuse, we can begin to understand the complex ways in which it affects women, but also the strengths that can emerge. All of these factors influenced the ways in which these women began to rebuild their lives, their ability to overcome successfully the challenges it faced them and to make a successful transition to independent living. The refuge and the support it provided enabled them to begin this process; the next stage was the offer of a new home.

Summary

- Domestic violence and abuse can take many forms, including physical, sexual, psychological, financial and emotional abuse. All of these elements are likely to feed on and reinforce each other, producing a state of constant fear and anxiety in those who experience them and a loss of any sense of physical and emotional safety.

- Although many of them had suffered major physical and sexual abuse, women said that it was the emotional abuse that had the greatest impact and long-term effect on them. It had destroyed their sense of self-worth and confidence, isolated them from potential sources of support, and made it very difficult for them to trust either themselves or other individuals or organisations.

- Despite the difficulties of their situation, the women did not see themselves as passive or helpless. They acted to protect themselves and their children, monitoring their own behaviour, managing the risks and doing their best to maintain links to others.

- Utilising Maslow's concept of human needs (Figure 1.1, page 23) offers a framework for understanding the way in which domestic violence affects individuals, destroying personal integrity, blocking communication with others and removing any concept of safety. This model recognises the way in which the women actively seek to influence their situation and their determination to improve the quality of their lives.

- Given the dangers inherent in leaving and the effect that abuse had had on their confidence, taking the decision to leave was immensely difficult, made more so by the conflicting emotions that women felt towards their abuser.

- In leaving, women lost not only the relationship in which they had invested so much of themselves, but also the bulk of their material possessions and a familiar environment. They recognised the significance of these multiple losses and the fact that they needed to deal with the pain and grief of this before they could move on with their lives. The refuge had provided safety and a supportive community where the women could start the process of recovery and rebuild their confidence.

- The allocation of a property marked the start of a new phase in their lives. Although a few women had been so traumatised by their experiences that they were unable to formulate a future for themselves, most had hopes and expectations about their new lives. They wanted a life free from violence, safety for themselves and their children, and the chance to make a new home that would remain intact. Some were looking even further ahead, for the opportunity to broaden their horizons and for personal achievement.

- The fears they expressed about their new lives were directly related to the effect that abuse had had on them: being alone, making decisions for themselves and, crucially, being found by their abuser, or by his or her family.

- At the same time, the women displayed a determination to make a success of their new lives, overcome the challenges they knew would face them, and make a successful transition to independent living.

Notes

1. Recent UK research (Robinson 2007) has shown that this intuitive assessment by women of the risk to themselves and their children and of alternative courses of action, such as leaving, is likely to be substantially accurate and needs to be fully taken into account by any supporting agencies.

2. Other researchers (Campbell et al. 1998; Dobash et al. 2000; Kirkwood 1993; Lempert 1996; Lowe, Humphreys and Williams 2007) have similarly noted positive coping strategies by women living in situations of domestic violence.

3. Maslow 1987 (first published 1954).

4. Povey et al. 2008.

5. The marked similarity of impact and the process of recovery between the losses experienced in bereavement and those resulting from domestic violence and abuse were examined in my earlier research (Abrahams 2007).

6. Abrahams 2007.

Chapter 2

The Transformation of Home

Home was a word with deep emotional significance for all the women; it meant far more to them than a roof over their heads or even a safe place to live with their children. While in the refuge, they had talked constantly to me of wanting 'a place of my own' and 'my own front door' – just how important it had been for them to fulfil this need was confirmed on my later visits, when women talked with immense pride and pleasure of the homes they had created. Turning hopes into realities, however, and moving from the refuge to holding a tenancy of their own was a long and often complex process. The first step was to think about where they were going to live: should they seek to return to their old homes, or to a new home in the same area; relocate near the refuge, or move to a completely different location? Once this decision had been made, they had to apply to the relevant organisations and authorities, keep checking on what was happening and be alert to any new opportunities for rehousing, while considering how to get the basic furniture and equipment that they would need. Moving house is, in itself, commonly regarded as one of the most stressful experiences in life for any individual to handle, and, for these women, there were additional stressors caused by the abuse to deal with – their low levels of self-esteem and confidence, and their fears about safety and independent living.

Once the move had taken place, however, a major shift in attitude seemed to begin to happen. When they had been in the abusive relationship, to adapt an old phrase, 'home was where the hurt was'. Now, it was a safe and precious space, where they could be creative without the risk of criticism or of having fabric and possessions destroyed by their abuser. Now, as they worked to transform their homes, a similar transformatory process seemed to take place within the women themselves, as they began to gain control over their environment, take decisions and make choices.

For two women, however, the converse was true. They had initially moved into permanent accommodation, but had been forced to move again because of unforeseen and destructive changes in their lives. For them, life had again become unsafe and unpredictable; the lack of a permanent home was making it hard to deal with other practical problems or their recovery from domestic violence and abuse.

Women and home

To understand why the concept of 'home' was so important to these women, we need to look back to how society has traditionally seen the role of women: primarily as homemakers and as the person responsible for raising children and, perhaps, caring for older or dependent relatives. This view, encapsulated in phrases like 'a woman's place is in the home', has also formed the basis for many past aspects of social policy.[1] It is hardly surprising, therefore, that, for generations of women, the home – their main workplace and often the only sphere of influence open to them – became a focus for their personal identity, central to their lives and sense of self.[2] Over the last 30 years, there have been many changes in the lives of women: they now comprise a major section of the workforce, many closed professions have been (theoretically) opened to them, and legislation intended to secure equality of treatment and opportunities has been promulgated. Yet, paradoxically, there are still expectations in society, which are reflected in TV and the press, that it is women who will both work and take the major share of creating homes and caring for children. This traditional role, and the sense of self related to it, remains the reality of most women's lives and was reflected in the way women talked to me about the homes they had created and the satisfaction they had gained from this. Gemma was, perhaps, an extreme example:

> I mean in my old home I did everything…most of the colours I did two-tone…and I could afford really expensive paints as well…and I always made sure that I'd matched the border. All the duvet covers were matching, everything was matching…even down to the mirrors, everything was absolutely perfect. The skirting board was slightly cream colour, to match with the hallway and the carpet…everything was absolutely matched in perfectly.

Controlling aspects of domestic abuse (discussed in Chapter 1) often centred around the standards and expectations that their partners had of how the home should be run. Any failure in this direction might well prove to be a trigger for abuse, so that this was even more of a reason to pour time and energy into perfecting their role. Even when their efforts to create a home were constantly criticised and undermined by their abuser, and their furniture and possessions trashed, home was still a place to which women felt immense attachment. It was a part of themselves and a way, however limited, in which they could express something of their own personalities. Taking the decision to leave it was, therefore, a devastating experience, adding yet another facet of loss to their lives.

Where shall I go?

Despite this deep attachment, however, none of the women wanted to return to their old homes. There were several interrelated factors behind this painful decision: first and foremost was the fear of what action the abuser, or his or her family, might do if they returned, even with the possibility of legally enforceable sanctions to protect them. Two women had, in fact, taken out injunctions against their partners after moving out, but these had been broken on several occasions, and although the police response had been helpful, the shock and distress that the incidents had caused had been so great that the women had decided to come to a refuge. In Briony's circumstances, it was the police themselves who had recommended this course of action. The general opinion among the women was that legal solutions were unlikely to be effective, and there was also a profound mistrust and reluctance to become involved with the legal system. In any case, the majority did not want to take personal legal action against their abuser, for whom they still had feelings of love and loyalty, but also fear of possible repercussions. If the abuser was also the father of one, or more, of their children, there was an added reluctance to take action that would criminalise him and perhaps jeopardise any future relationship with his children.[3]

A further emotional barrier to returning to their former homes was the fact that this was where the abuse had taken place. Previously, they had concentrated on the positive aspects of their home, as a way of blocking out the abuse. Now, although they were mourning the loss of their home, the unhappy memories it held were also clear in their minds.[4] They also feared the stigma that they felt might be attached to them and their children if they returned. Sylvia was apprehensive as to what her partner might attempt, but even more nervous about the long-term aspects of what the neighbours might say. This would affect not only her, but also her teenage daughters and their relationships with their friends, including possible boyfriends:

It was a little close of about 20 houses. It was very quiet, but unfortunately that was one of the main reasons to move, because not only did [he] know where we were…and we were quite vulnerable on the little close, but also the talk on the close and things like that, you know. It was not nice…there's not many people know the full ins and outs and implications of what happened, and I didn't want them to know either, because I didn't want any kind of whispering and stigmas and things. I don't think I'd ever have felt safe there. I don't think I'd ever have felt I had a real friend, even though they were my friends. I'd have always felt that, behind closed doors…when I wasn't about, I'd have been a subject.

Despite campaigns to increase the understanding of and support for those who experience domestic violence and abuse, this is still not a topic for open discussion, and myths about women being, in some way, responsible for the abuse are still commonly held. Sylvia's fears may well have been justified; on the other hand, her neighbours might have proved understanding and supportive. What was clear, however, was that her feelings of shame and guilt had been internalised and that this was continuing to place a barrier between her and her neighbours, reinforcing her fear of trusting others.

It often took a considerable time for women to come to terms with their sadness and sense of loss at not being able to go back to an environment, places and people they knew, and for them to feel emotionally ready to move on.[5] They then had to consider the options available: to stay within the catchment area of the refuge and its community support services, or move to another locality, where these services might not be available. Considerations might also include being near to other support services, including potentially supportive members of the family, the availability of housing, access to public transport, schools, shopping facilities or services for children with special medical or educational needs. They also had to consider safety and the likelihood of being found by their abuser. This was not necessarily a case of geographical distance, but of patterns of transport, the village-like nature of communities within larger cities and the natural grouping of towns within a district.

Initially, eight women settled in the same large city or major town as the refuge and within twelve miles of their old homes, but in a different community. This meant that they had a broad knowledge of the area already and could access refuge support, but they felt reasonably secure from any chance encounter with their abuser. Four women had moved much longer distances to reach safety (one had travelled over 300 miles) and had decided to settle in the locality. One of these women was, in fact, returning to the town she had been brought up in, but the others had no knowledge of what were good or bad areas and needed to explore for themselves, rather than take the risk of being allocated somewhere that felt unsafe. Briony took to the road:

> I got a day saver and just got on the buses and just went round. And then my friend [from the refuge] moved, so I got to know that area pretty well, and then we went up to Sainsbury's on the bus and I saw all this area, so I put that down as well. So it's a case of get on the bus and have a look round, which is what I did. 'Cos I thought, if I'm going to live here, I might as well have a look around and find nice areas to live.

Getting a property

None of the women had access to savings, or other financial resources; in fact, two of them were already in debt from rent arrears incurred in their names and damage to property caused by their partners. Only one of them had a job to go to when she left the refuge and, although this was reasonably well paid, there was no lump sum available for a deposit, and a mortgage would have been an unsustainable burden on her finances. All of them were, therefore, reliant on social housing provision from Local Authority stock or, increasingly, from Housing Associations. The application process was different in each area and women had to be proactive in their approaches to the agencies involved. Sylvia said:

> Seven months. I hadn't had a single offer of property in all that time, not one. And that was going down every week, doing all the business. I must have been a member of every association going. But there was just nothing, there was nothing at all. And, as I say, this one came up eventually, but it absolutely needed gutting. But it was a case of, well, I've got to take it because you know [the refuge] can't keep me here really. ...You know, 'cos they've got ladies waiting. You can imagine, can't you, seven months in a place with nothing of your own around you.

In addition to the time and effort spent in physically chasing up their applications, an immense amount of emotional energy was needed to keep them going during this process, at a time when they were still in a state of shock and grieving for the losses they had sustained. It was also hard for women whose self-esteem and confidence were at an extremely low level to put themselves forward in the way that appeared to be necessary if they were to get rehoused. Like Sylvia, Lindy had also been a refuge resident for seven months and mirrored the general feeling of frustration and increasing depression when women felt they were ready to move on and no property became available despite all their efforts.

> Far too long. Just want to get...the way I'd describe it is like being stuck in welly boots full of concrete. You get to a certain...you start progressing and getting yourself...'Right, I've got that stage of my life done and that's sorted' and then you're like...can't get any further. You're stuck. I just hate it.

Although three other women had been rehoused after less than four months in the refuge, five had had to wait for periods of up to six months for an offer. Briony had succeeded in moving out 364 days after first entering a refuge, but Jeannie had waited in refuge accommodation for 19 months before being rehoused. These extended refuge stays were not typical – they had arisen, in both cases, from considerations of personal safety, which had forced them to move a considerable distance from one refuge to another. This further delayed the start of the rehousing process and also made it difficult for them to reach a decision on where they wanted to settle.[6]

Often the frustration that women like Sylvia and Lindy experienced led to them taking properties that were in very bad condition or 'hard to let' because of their poor location or other unattractive features. Four of them thought that they had been extremely fortunate in the properties they had eventually been offered, but they, in common with all of the others, felt that they had had very limited or no choice as to what they were offered and that little attention had been paid to any specific needs they might have. Maddy, for example, who had chronic leg problems and limited mobility, had initially been placed by the local authority in a second-floor maisonette that had no lift, and had suffered from anti-social behaviour directed at her. With the help of the refuge support worker, she had, very quickly, been able to relocate to a more accessible property, on a small, low-cost, development of new houses. This was a private let, and the support worker commented that to find affordable property of this nature was very difficult. This whole situation – the delays, the frustrations, the feeling that they were second-class citizens whose needs were not a priority – further impacted on their already low feelings of self-worth.[7]

A further source of stress and anxiety lay in the fact that, once a property had been offered, women found that they were expected to make up their minds immediately and sign a tenancy agreement, often on the same day. There was little time to think things over or to look round the actual locality of the property, and women who were already frustrated at their inability to move out were nervous that turning down an offer might prejudice future opportunities. An added complication was that, once they had signed for the property, they became liable for the rent, plus that for their refuge accommodation. Only one housing benefit was payable in respect of the family and, if women needed to wait for a community care grant before they could move, they were liable to incur a degree of debt to start their new lives. Keira's had been a typical experience:

> While I felt very lucky that I'd got a property, the minute I looked at it, I had to sign for it, which then made me responsible for the rent. So I'd got, at that time, £57.10 a week accruing. And all the time I was living at [the refuge] I couldn't afford to pay for it. The council...housing benefit would only pay for one accommodation, so I actually moved in here in debt to start with. So that's not a good thing, is it?

As Davis (2003) points out in her study of Housing Associations, this pressure to take up accommodation stems from the need for social landlords to maximise rental streams and to avoid houses that remain vacant for long periods becoming subject to vandalism. Although entirely understandable, there is no doubt that the dual responsibility and the rush to view, sign and then move, after all the frustration and delay, caused additional emotional stress for the women involved.

Condition and maintenance

On their initial move, five women had been allocated property with a housing association. Maddy, after her brief spell in a council maisonette, had moved to a private landlord, and another woman to a private let via the council. Although these properties were all in reasonable condition, the five families who moved into council-owned property found that they were in poor repair.[8] For Leanne, it was a life-threatening problem:

> The day we were supposed to move in, Nigel [her young son] came running into the living room and went crashing through the floorboards. And water, there was water under the house like, this deep – electric cables all over the place. How I didn't electrocute myself I don't know. But anyway, so we had to move out again and back into a bed and breakfast for 18 weeks while they did damp proof and got all the water out and concreted it all. It was awful.

In discussing repairs and maintenance to these properties, there was general agreement that the council service was poor: slow, with long delays before any action was taken, and inefficient, with half-completed jobs being a frequent complaint. And, as in other situations, it could be difficult for women with low confidence to maintain the pressure and persistence necessary to get problems rectified on their own. Housing Associations were generally considered good, although there were a few comments on delays in responding on some occasions.

Despite all the problems they had experienced in accessing accommodation, moving in and maintaining their new homes, once they had lived there for a few years, the women said that they were generally pleased (and sometimes 'very happy') with where they lived. Much of this pleasure derived from the way they had worked on the process of creating an environment that was entirely their own.

It's mine!

Most women had left with just what they could carry, or put in the car, if they had one. Charmian and Maddy, who had both walked out with nothing, had gone back, with a police escort, to get whatever they could, in what felt to them like a five-minute 'window of opportunity'. 'I got stuff…just grabbed what I could, basically, and went out the house and stuffed it in the car,' said Maddy. Furniture and household equipment had had to be left behind in most cases, although two women had been able to get their furniture and possessions into storage near their old homes, to recover later. Consequently, when women were allocated a property, the majority were starting from an extremely low base. Community care grants were inconsistent[9] both within and between localities, and often payment was considerably delayed, so that women had to wait to buy even the most basic equipment to start with. Given the mounting debt she was incurring, Keira decided to move as soon as her grant had arrived so that she could buy beds and bedding for her children and get them delivered. 'So I moved…and I moved without a cooker, without a bed for myself… without any real furniture. And I moved in here and slept on the floor for two weeks.'

Liz found that, due to a malicious phone call, she was unable to get the community care grant and had to rely on the few items that donations to the refuge had provided. Nevertheless, she was determined not to let this get in the way of moving into her new home:

When I did come to put in for a community grant, I didn't get one, because they said somebody had phoned up and said that I'd already got furniture in storage [but] I didn't have nothing. So I had to start from scratch with nothing. Just had a mattress and some kitchen utensils to start with…but we'd got an 'ouse!

Even with the most careful budgeting and a reasonable community care grant, women needed to rely on second-hand furniture and white goods to equip their new homes to a minimum level. In some areas, there are voluntary agencies that collect and recycle furniture and furnishings, which can be bought at low prices. Leanne went to one of these: 'I just got standard stuff from a furniture warehouse store. You know, like second-hand furniture. You pay a certain amount…they're good.' These provisions are not universal, however, and many, like Charmian, relied on the generosity of family and friends to help them out:

Oh my friends were great. Yeah, my mate Di came down…my mate Pat came. Um…Di, she gave me the carpet. My mate Gina gave me the three-piece suite. My uncle Bill gave me the telly, computer. My mate gave me the fish tank. I've had fridge and freezer given. The only thing I bought was the beds and my washing machine and my cooker. But now I'm starting to save up and replace things as I'm going along. So that they're mine and not what other people have had.

Whether they had eventually managed to get their goods out of store, relied on charity shop purchases, or had been grateful for gifts from friends, burning desire to replace other people's cast-offs or reminders of an unhappy past with goods of their own choice existed among all the women. In doing this, they were learning to make decisions and exercise their right to choose – opportunities that had been denied them in the past. At the same time, they were making a very positive statement about the way in which they were beginning to value themselves – not as 'second hand', but as individuals who were worthy of having new and attractive possessions. And the fact that they felt safe in their new environment meant that they could risk buying things, knowing that their new possessions would not be destroyed by violence, or, as in Leanne's case, sold to feed her partner's drug habit.

The telly's on a pound meter. It's summat I never would have been able to have before, 'cos it would have been cut off and sold…well, emptied…and then the telly gone…and DVDs and CDs, I can have them and they won't go missing.

A further important aspect to the growth of self-worth was the scope to paint and decorate their new home to their own taste. In every interview there were comments that this was what had made the new property feel like it was their home. In choosing colours, changing their minds and redecorating, they were acknowledging the way they were changing. When I first met Briony, she told me that her husband had had firm views on what colour was appropriate in the home and had insisted on magnolia for everything. On my second visit, she was experimenting with pastels, but on the final visit there were patches of bright colour everywhere, as she tried to decide on what she liked best. The only colour missing from the walls was – magnolia! For many of them, this form of creativity was also a way of proving their abusers wrong and that they were capable of doing things for themselves. Charmian's partner had told her that she was incapable of decorating a room by herself; she had now repainted the entire house, to her immense satisfaction, refusing any help, including that from her mother:

> And she didn't like it. But I says, 'No, this is my challenge and it's me that's going to do it.' I'm going to say, 'I've done it', instead of saying, 'Oh, my mum did that, my mum did that room.' It's not something I wanted to do. I wanted to do it myself, without any help. And I did!

And for Lindy, DIY gave her a pride that she had not experienced before: 'I decorated it myself from top to bottom. I hung the lamps and changed plugs and… It's mine. It's not a man's. It's mine!'

Many local authorities and housing associations will provide either money or vouchers to assist with the cost of redecorating, if a property is deemed to be in bad decorative order, but not in need of major repair work (which would be carried out by their employees or contractors and would also include redecorating). Only one woman was able to take advantage of this provision, but, given the emotional importance that women attached to this process, in terms of making a home their own, a more flexible approach might be a way of helping the family to settle in at comparatively small outlay.

Settling in, moving on

Over the years that I had been interviewing them, there had, not surprisingly, been a few changes in residences. Sally had moved to a larger Housing Association property in the same town, in order to provide more space for her own and her current partner's children. She was one of the two women who had accumulated substantial debts in rent arrears and the cost of repairing damage to their previous homes. These arrears, which were not her fault, but for which she was deemed responsible, had not hampered her initial rehousing and she had been making small weekly repayments. In needing to move to a different property, however, she was required to make a significant reduction in the amount outstanding, which she and her partner managed to do, with help from family members. Her remaining debt is continuing to be cleared by weekly payments. Lindy, although sad to leave the house into which she had put such love and care, had found a new partner and they now own their own property on an estate close to her original home.

Two women were hoping to move again shortly after our last interview. Charmian felt she wanted a more rural environment, as her existing locality became more built up, but she was happy to remain where she was until something suitable became available. Molly, who had achieved so much in the time since she left the refuge, had developed life-threatening heart problems (unconnected with the abuse) and needed to move to specially adapted housing.

But for Jeannie and Gemma, their initial hopes on moving to permanent accommodation had not been realised. Jeannie, whose euphoria on finding a house was seen in Chapter 1, had taken a private let via the council. As she later realised, in her excitement at finally getting a property, she had not asked enough questions, nor fully understood the terms of the let or the long-term implications for her benefits: 'I was just such…you know, when you're just so, like, fired up. I didn't even really ask questions and I didn't know where I stood.' She became unable to pay the rent after twelve months and was eventually taken to court and evicted. Now homeless, her situation was made more complex because she had come to feel 'out of place' in the locality where she had been rehoused and wanted to move to an area controlled by a different local authority. Historically, there has been extreme reluctance on the part of councils to agree to this, and Jeannie felt that, without the hard work of Shelter and the refuge, she would not have been able to make this move. Until she was officially accepted as homeless, she spent several weeks staying with family and friends (often referred to as 'hidden' homelessness) before being placed in bed and breakfast accommodation in her chosen area. Her application to be permanently rehoused there was still under consideration at the time of our last talk.

Gemma had originally settled in a Housing Association property, but had become enmeshed in a further violent relationship (discussed more fully in Chapter 4) and eventually decided her only option was to leave and go to another refuge, a long way from her home. She then found she was again pregnant by her abuser and, in the shock and distress this caused her, she returned to drinking to excess, one of the mechanisms she had used before to numb the pain of abuse. The workers felt that they were no longer able to support her within the refuge and that her presence was not helpful to other residents.[10] She was initially placed in bed and breakfast accommodation and then moved into a council property on a temporary basis. Meanwhile, her children had been taken into care, pending further consideration of their best interests.

For both women, life had, yet again, become unpredictable and unsafe. They were never sure if, or when, they were going to have to move on again, perhaps at short notice, and saw no point in investing time and energy in their temporary accommodation. Nor did they feel able to get involved in the community around them, or to consider studying or looking for employment. Jeannie talked about the stress this caused her and how she yearned for her own space:

> I'm still actually homeless. I'm still classed as homeless. The lady comes every week. She has to come to check that I'm still here and I've got to sign this paper. And also the council can just come here at any time, day or night, spontaneously, just to check that I'm here and there's no one else living here. I just hope that, eventually, I'll just get somewhere that I can call my own. And then my kids will be settled, I'll be settled, whether it's work or studying, and just looking forward to the future, seeing my kids grow up.

At the time of my earlier interviews with Jeannie and Gemma, they had moved into their new homes and were beginning to think constructively about the future. Now, although both women were clearly doing their best to hold things together and be positive about their long-term outcomes, their emerging self-worth and confidence had been adversely affected and delayed the process of recovery from domestic violence and abuse.

Their situation was in stark contrast to all of the other women (with the exception of Molly) who had remained in their permanent accommodation. Instead of being the place where they lived in fear, trapped by their abuser, home was now a creative space, and the process of building up their homes, choosing furniture and redecorating to their own taste, had begun to rebuild their confidence in their own abilities and a sense of pride in their homes and in themselves. Importantly, they were also beginning to feel safe, although an undercurrent of fear and anxiety would be running through their lives for many years to come. They had faced, and overcome, what had seemed at the time to be major difficulties, and they were beginning to realise that they could take decisions, that they were in control of their lives now and that there were choices open to them. At times, this complete change from the abusive situation was to prove overwhelming, but over the period of this study, I watched them learning to cope.

Although the move to a new home was the essential foundation for this transformatory process, the women acknowledged that, without help and support from refuge services based in the community, they would have had greater difficulties in overcoming their fears – being alone, taking decisions and building a new life. Many other research studies[11] have emphasised the crucial importance of safe, suitable and permanent accommodation for women who have experienced domestic violence and abuse, and the need for this to be coupled with appropriate support services, providing both practical information and, equally importantly, emotional support. Together, housing and support begin to provide the basic building blocks of Maslow's ideas on human need – safety and the opportunity for women to build support networks and find a place in the community around them.

Summary

- The concept of 'home' was of central importance to the women, providing a focus for their personal identity and sense of self. Taking the decision to leave it added to their feelings of grief and loss.

- Fear of their abuser and his or her family, unhappy memories of the place where the abuse took place and the possibility of gossip and innuendo among the neighbours meant that they did not want to return to their old homes. Even where legal protection might have been possible, women were doubtful about its effectiveness. They were mistrustful of the legal system in general and were also reluctant to criminalise their partner by instigating legal action. This was particularly true if the abuser was also the father of one, or more, of their children.

- Considerations of where to live included access to support services, including those of the refuge, local schools, transport and shops.

Safety was of prime importance, but this was not necessarily a case of geographical distance from the abuser.

- All of the women were reliant on social housing, with time-consuming and complex application procedures. It was difficult for women with low confidence and still in a state of shock to pursue their applications vigorously, and they became frustrated and depressed during the process.

- Inability to obtain reasonable accommodation within a realistic timescale has been identified as the single most significant barrier preventing women from leaving abusive relationships, and frustration and failure to be rehoused may well drive them back to their abuser.

- Women felt that little attention had been paid to their specific needs with regard to safety, physical mobility and accessibility. Properties were often in a poor state of repair, even before they moved in, and maintenance was slow. Pressure to accept a tenancy and sign for it immediately meant that they became responsible for the rent as well as that due to the refuge. As a result, many women started their new lives in debt.

- Community care grants (to enable women to buy basic furniture and equipment) were inconsistent in their application, and there were often long delays in making payment. In some areas, recycled furniture and white goods are available from voluntary agencies at minimal cost, but these provisions are not universally available. The women often had to rely on donations from friends or from the refuge.

- Replacing donated goods with items of their own choosing and redecorating their new homes enabled women to develop their sense of autonomy and build their confidence in making choices and taking decisions.

- Where women had had to move on again, after being rehoused, into bed and breakfast premises or into housing used as temporary accommodation, they felt insecure, reluctant to invest emotionally in the community around them or to plan for their future. This further damaged their confidence and self-esteem and delayed their recovery from the abuse.

- The provision of housing alone was not sufficient to enable women to sustain their own tenancy. Practical and emotional support was also needed as they began to develop new networks. Together, housing and support begin to provide the basic building blocks of Maslow's ideas on human need – safety and the potential for women to build support networks and find a place in the community around them.

Notes

1. For example, the Beveridge Report of 1942, which led to the founding of the Welfare State, was predicated on the concept of a male wage earner and a wife at home, or, at best, as a secondary wage earner, whose primary responsibilities lay in the home (Deacon 1995).

2. Malos and Hague (1997) point out that, traditionally, men spend more time outside the home and that it serves a different purpose in their lives, being seen as a setting primarily for leisure and relaxation, as opposed to a place of work.

3. Taking legal action against the perpetrators of domestic abuse is a key part of the government's strategy on tackling violence against women. There have been major changes to the criminal justice system since these women first left the refuge, including new legislation and the introduction of Special Domestic Violence Courts (SDVCs) and funding for Independent Domestic Violence Advisors (IDVAs). (IDVAs are specially trained and qualified individuals who work with and support those at high risk of harm to assess the levels of risk, discuss the range of suitable options – which may include civil or criminal proceedings – and develop safety plans. CAADA 2009.) This might have resulted in different decisions being made by the women, where this type of legal action was a possibility. An early evaluation of the Domestic Violence, Crime and Victims Act 2004, however (Hester *et al.* 2008), suggests that there has been a drop in applications to courts for non-molestation orders. They postulate that this may be due to reduced access to legal aid, or the fact that breaches of these orders can now carry criminal penalties, including imprisonment. This may well link to the views expressed by the women in this study on their reluctance to see the perpetrator imprisoned and with a criminal record. Similar comments have been made by a senior judge (Platt 2008).

4. Malos and Hague (1997) also comment on a reluctance to return to the family home after the events that have taken place there.

5. None of the refuges in the study was able to offer, at that time, the option of move-on accommodation, which provides women with a space to adjust to living independently in a new locality, but with the advantage of easy access to the refuge and its services. This provision also relieves the pressure on the emergency accommodation of the refuge. The disadvantage, however, may lie in

the need to move on again, thus delaying the time when women are able to settle permanently.

6. Previous research (Abrahams 2007) indicated that there was a risk of women who were too long resident in a refuge becoming institutionalised. This was not the situation here – both women were desperate to become independent again as the disadvantages of refuge life began to bear more heavily.

7. Being able to obtain suitable accommodation of a reasonable standard, within a realistic timescale, has been identified for decades as being the single most significant obstacle to women leaving an abusive relationship. Not only does it stop them leaving, but it may also drive those who do take this step back to the abuser in frustration and despair (Binney, Harkell and Nixon 1981; Charles 1994; Davis 2003; Dobash and Dobash 1992; Malos and Hague 1993).

8. The government's policy statement 'The Way Forward for Housing', published in 2001, set a target for all social housing to meet a decent standard by 2010. ('Decent' requires meeting minimum housing standards, being in a reasonable state of repair, warm, weatherproof and with reasonably modern facilities and services.) Major strides have been made by social landlords in upgrading properties, and it is anticipated that 95 per cent will be met by the target date (Communities and Local Government 2009).

9. The research carried out for the Office of the Deputy Prime Minister (now Communities and Local Government) found 'inconsistent disparities in the value of a care grant awarded to service users in apparently similar circumstances, which were not understood by either staff or service users' (Supporting People 2007, p.19).

10. Women who experience domestic violence and also have mental health problems and/or alcohol and/or drug dependencies have complex support needs (Barron 2004) and refuge workers reported that they were encountering an increasing number of women with multiple problems of this nature. Major efforts are being made, in some areas, to provide the additional resources and training to meet this situation, but, although some refuges are able to work with these women and have specially trained support staff, many provide shared facilities, which may not always be suitable for the needs of this group, and limited resources for offering the higher level of support that may be required.

11. For example, Charles 1994; Jones, Pleace and Quilgars 2002; McNaughton 2005.

Chapter 3

Building Support Systems

When women leave abusive relationships and seek safety in refuges or other safe accommodation, they tear themselves and their children out of the regulatory and support systems in which most of us are embedded and take for granted: the services run by their local authority, from libraries to schools and electoral registers, access to a GP, health visitor or other NHS services, dentists, opticians, nurseries and childcare. Some of these links – registration with a local doctor, schools for their children – might have to be made on a temporary basis while in the refuge; others, such as benefit and housing support, needed to be initiated, if they have never been accessed before, or renegotiated in the changed circumstances.

As the women moved into their new tenancies, these links needed to change again and additional ones established, as they started to set up their own households and arrange for the services that would enable them to live there – utilities such as gas, electricity, water, council services – and contact with other support agencies. For eight of the women, this was the first time they had held a tenancy in their names alone, and having to apply for services, complete application forms and coordinate everything was a challenge. This was particularly so when, while in the relationship, they had been forbidden to organise things or constantly told they were inadequate. Even those who had previously had their own homes, or had experience of how businesses and organisations worked, felt, to some extent, nervous of their immediate ability to carry out these tasks alone. This was, in part, due to the negative effects of the abuse, but also because, during their time in the refuge, housing, and all the services associated with this, had been provided for them and they had not had to take on this responsibility. Now they were stepping out again and it felt strange and bewildering.

Having the support of a worker whom they knew and trusted, therefore, to guide them at the start of their new lives, was a service that they had valued highly. Assisting women successfully to establish new support networks with agencies and organisations and, perhaps, to regain contact with their families were key elements in helping women to settle in their new communities. Above all, this support was directed at giving them the confidence and skills to control their own lives for the longer-term future.

Working together

The first priority of most refuge groups in the past has generally been to provide emergency accommodation for women and children who are escaping abusive relationships, and this has also been seen as a key service by newer organisations working in this area (such as housing associations). Although some women will have gained sufficient strength and confidence from the support they received during their stay in the refuge to go out and establish new lives on their own, it has always been accepted that the majority will need some form of support, both as they move back into the community and for some time afterwards. As always, the ability to provide this support has been constricted by lack of financial resources, and, previously, many groups had only been able to provide telephone support at this crucial stage. Support in the community has gradually become more readily available, although there are still major gaps in the provision of all services for those who experience domestic violence and abuse.[1] At the time that they first left the refuge, ten of the women were able to access personal support provided by the refuge, specifically to assist them in settling into their new community.[2]

This support was not in any way shapeless or aimless. Once rehousing was becoming a possibility, the worker would sit down with the woman and explain what support was available. Together, they would discuss her aims, objectives and goals, the degree of support needed and how this might best be given, and then formulate a support plan. This would include a full risk assessment and safety plans for the woman and her children.[3] The way in which support was provided needed to be flexible, taking into account both the changing pattern of needs and the woman's own capabilities; visits at agreed intervals, telephone contact and being with the woman as she made contact with other agencies were often part of the package. Whatever approach was adopted, it was vital that support was consistent and reliable, in contrast to the situation during the abuse and to avoid any feeling of revictimisation. Both the risk assessment and the support plan were continually reassessed and changed if necessary to reflect the reality of the situation and the progress being made.

Support from the refuge was designed to be intensive for a short period of time (which varied, depending on need, but was usually not longer than six months) and then tapering off as the woman built up confidence and established other support systems. Crucial for the success of this support plan was that women saw themselves as active participants in this process and were clear about the boundaries and limitations of the support.

Dealing with the nuts and bolts

Practical assistance and information were the most obvious elements of the support that the women needed. This ranged from detailed knowledge of the local statutory services and agencies and assisting women to make contact with them, to knowing where they could find cheap furniture and essential electrical equipment. Where the new accommodation was not habitable, workers had the contacts and confidence, which the women initially lacked, to get things put right. For example, Leanne, whose major problems with her property were discussed in Chapter 2, did not have the confidence, at that stage of her life, to tackle problems like this on her own. She needed the active involvement of the refuge worker to enable her to move into her new home:

> Well… Let's put it this way…she kicked council up their arse! Because it would have taken a lot longer, but she was ringing up all the time and how was this doing, how was that doing? And we came to view it when they were halfway through it. And she picked up one of their checklists and she was checking it. And she said, 'Well, they haven't done that properly' and 'I'm complaining about this'. And she was brilliant.

Having worked alongside the refuge worker on this and other practical problems, Leanne was now able to sort out problems for herself and felt a lot more confident in dealing with these situations: 'Like you can't fluff around. You…say it how it is.'

Building the capacity to cope

Although advocacy[4] of this nature was often needed to begin with, empowering women to be able to take action for themselves was the long-term aim. To do this, it was necessary not simply to provide information and practical knowledge, but also to build up confidence and self-esteem and to encourage women as they tried out new skills and ways of being and explored new opportunities. Given the damaging effects that abuse had often had on their belief in themselves and their abilities, this was not a straightforward process; they would begin to gain confidence and move forward, then be pushed back by a perceived failure and need to pick themselves up and start again. One of the important factors in this process of support was the fact that women knew the worker, so that they did not have to repeat their story again and already felt they could trust and relate to her. Because workers fully understood the physical and emotional effects of domestic violence, they were able to listen to and understand the concerns of the women, without judging them. If it appeared necessary, however, they were fully prepared to take up a bracing and challenging approach.

All of the women who received help on their initial moves spoke positively about their support worker and valued the way she had built up their confidence and self-respect. Jeannie said, 'She really made me believe in myself again,' and Liz had seen, in her support worker, a role model for her own future: 'I saw summat in her that I wanted to be. You know, a proud woman.' Women were very clear as to what aspects of their approach had been helpful to them:

- Having just one person whose prime concern was them and their children.

- Being treated with respect.

- Being shown choices and options, but staying in control. 'She's brilliant like that,' said Sylvia. 'She doesn't give you answers, she doesn't tell you what to do, but she gives you feedback.'

- Being helped to stand on their own feet and make decisions.

- Taking a flexible approach as to how support was given – Sally said, 'She's there for us if we need her' – but not pushing it if they were managing fine.

Moments of uncertainty

There were two 'pinch points' when women said that they felt at their most vulnerable and isolated. One was on the first night in their new homes, after the door had closed behind any helpers and they were alone with their children. Most of them had been warned that they would probably sit down and cry, both from the relief that they had actually made it to this point and from a feeling of having taken on an overwhelming responsibility. In the excitement of moving in, this had been forgotten, and the reaction, when it occurred, was devastating. Lindy, who, in Chapter 1, recalled being warned of what might happen, was no exception: 'I remember the first night shutting that door. I do remember crying, but... 'cos it was oh my God, it's all down to me now.'

The second high stress point, particularly in the early days, came in the evenings and at night, once they had put their children to bed and they were on their own. This was a time when unexpected noises indoors, or in the street outside, would feel threatening; fears and memories of their previous experiences could come flooding back, making them feel anxious and vulnerable and increasing their feelings of loneliness and isolation. In the refuge there would generally have been at least one other adult around to talk things over with or to answer the door with them if they felt frightened. Here, there was no one.

It was at times like these that they would have liked to call someone for a chat and reassurance. Sylvia commented:

> I would say that little ball of, probably, a month or so transition is the hardest. And maybe where you perhaps could do with a hotline number, you know, that you could just pick up 24 hours a day and say, 'I'm really having a day where it's not going well, and, you know, and I waited till the kids have gone to bed and now I'm falling apart.' And someone's on the other end to say, like, you know, 'This is only today...and tomorrow... Take a deep breath, cleansing breath and everything will be fine', you know.

As other researchers have documented,[5] these feelings of loneliness and isolation are widespread among newly rehoused individuals. Although I noted, like Humphreys and Thiara (2002), that these feelings lessened after the first six months or so, they were certainly an initial concern for many of the women in this study. Unfortunately, as discussed in the next chapter, these early feelings may have played a part in the development of new and unhelpful relationships or in a return to previous partners.

Women felt they should have been able to cope; they wanted to protect the free time of their support worker and were reluctant to 'trouble' (their words) the helpline, when they were aware that there were women who desperately needed to do so, and whose lives, perhaps as theirs had been, would be put at risk by a delay in making contact. In fact, at the time of writing, the 24 hour National Helpline (see Appendix 3) was available to them and not heavily in use at these times.[6] Yet it appeared that the women were still being held back by the values put on them by their abuser: that they and their needs were not important and that they were, in some way, not worthy of being listened to. Of course, talking to a helpline worker can never be the same as talking to someone you know and trust, but it might have helped in combating these fears. Two women specifically said that warning them of these difficulties in advance was not enough; they would have liked more specific advice and guidance, while in the refuge, on dealing with the emotional stresses involved.[7] Whether this would be remembered later is uncertain; teaching coping strategies might be useful, but might not provide the emotional contact these women were seeking. An alternative may lie in the creation of more self-help and support groups (discussed further in Chapter 4), whose members share the same experiences and can offer mutual support, such as women had experienced in the refuge.[8]

Saying goodbye

As women began to settle into their new homes, practical and emotional support gradually tapered off. It was extremely difficult to find out when contractual support finally stopped; the women could not remember after such a long gap and it seemed that workers would often keep a minimal degree of contact with service users who, they felt, needed support for a while longer, even though they were not officially on their books. It was apparent, however, that most women, despite some inner misgivings, had felt ready to 'go it alone' after a period ranging from six to twelve months. Despite being aware, from the outset, that support was temporary and would cease at some stage, the reality of saying goodbye was hard and, for some, quite traumatic. Many commented that they suddenly felt they had lost a friend. They recognised that the worker had many other women needing her support, and several berated themselves for being selfish in wanting contact to continue. They also knew that they now had other sources of support and that, if necessary, the services of the refuge group were only a phone call away. Nevertheless, set in the context of the losses they had already suffered, losing the company of a person who had seen them through so much was like yet another bereavement, and they needed a little while to come to terms with the initial impact of the loss, adjust and move on.

Some groups have tried innovative ways of enabling women to maintain as much contact as they feel they need by creating drop-in centres, holding regular coffee mornings and opening women's centres. In this way, women can visit, meet up with current and former residents, staff and volunteers, discuss problems and receive informal low-level and peer support, without the need for higher-level interventions. Coffee mornings had been introduced in one of the groups and the women from that area appreciated the fact that it was there and that they could attend if they wished. There was certainly common agreement among all the women that some form of low-level support should be in place for those women who needed it and that this should be available for a far longer period, as Briony indicated:

> So the support when you leave, it's really... There should be a lot more support. Should be for your first year. I think it should be a lot longer than that, to be honest. I mean specially with some women... I mean I actually pride myself I'm a pretty strong person anyway. Can be very single-minded but I'm a strong person at times. You know but...like everybody, things do get me down. But...there's a lot of women that have gone through a lot worse than what we did, and the support's just not there for them. It should be long-term support, not twelve month maximum. And then, 'Right, you're on your own now.' There should be support things there for other people.

For two women, formal support arrangements were not in place at the time they had left the refuge. Both had felt more than ready to move on and cope with the practicalities of their situation (although they commented that someone with local knowledge and advice would have eased the process) and had also felt, before leaving, that they were capable of handling any emotional turmoil. They had come to realise, however, that a degree of emotional support would have been of great help, particularly during the early weeks and months. As Keira said:

> At the time when you're moving and you're coming into a new area, you've got schools to sort out for your children, doctors, dentists... just the whole practical side of things. I went through a lot of stress, I think, at that time and then, sort of, being told, 'Well, right, that's it, we've done as much as we can for you. Now, off you go.' So that... yes, it added to my stress, yes, it did add to my stress.

A support service had been set up subsequently in these areas and both women had been contacted to see if they were in need of help. This was some six months down the line, and they felt that they had got over the initial impact of rehousing and independent living and did not need further assistance. This change of view on the need for support after leaving has been found to apply to other women, and some groups have instituted a routine phone call to check back with them after a few weeks to see how things are going and if support is needed.

Help from the police

Although not normally seen primarily as a support service, members of the police had become involved in assisting six of the women immediately either prior to or just after leaving the abusive relationship. Women reported that they felt listened to and taken seriously; most of the officers were seen as having been supportive and helpful, with a degree of understanding of the problems and impact of domestic violence and abuse. (There were a number of comments contrasting the support on this occasion with that encountered on previous occasions.) The police have received considerable criticism in the past for their attitude towards domestic violence and have been making strenuous efforts to improve in this area.[9] These comments are welcome evidence that changes are beginning to filter through; it has to be recognised, however, that this was a small sample and that these officers were likely to have been members of the local Domestic Violence Unit (DVU) who would have received special training.

Approaching other agencies

Half of the women had approached, or become involved with, other statutory agencies and organisations during the period of the abuse; all of them had done so during their time in the refuge and for two thirds of them, this contact had continued subsequently. These included housing and benefits agencies, Social Services, medical and educational professionals. In general, their view of these agencies was very negative, in some cases amounting to fear and profound mistrust.

There were a number of reasons for this: first, any memories of how past approaches had been received and a fear of further rejection. Although some of them had encountered individual members of staff who had gone out of their way to understand and be helpful, this had not automatically been the case, and women had often felt that their personal needs were not being taken seriously and they felt intimidated and put down. Lindy was told, after a failed suicide attempt:

'Well, I've got your file in front of me, you've been offered no aftercare, it was decided you're getting no aftercare. ...You've got marriage problems; you need to seek legal advice.' You know, I'm screaming for help...and it was, like, 'Well, we can't help you, off you go.' ...I was just, 'I'm really screaming for help, but it's not coming.'

Eventually, she was given a telephone number for 'homelessness' and, in marked contrast, 'she was absolutely fantastic', putting Lindy in touch with the local refuge worker.

An additional factor was the lack of confidence and self-esteem, resulting from the denigration and criticism they had experienced. Women had been taught that they were not worth listening to and, as a result, they tended either to remain silent or to 'fire up' when their feelings of frustration and anger became too much to contain. Liz explained:

In these places, you just feel you're nothing and so, sometimes, you just keep...you might as well shut up, because you think you're not going to get listened to, so you just let everything ride and then things get worse and worse and worse, so then you burst. And then it escalates and you think, 'Boy, that's pathetic. Why didn't you just say something in the first place?'

Neither action was likely to produce a positive result, and the problem was exacerbated if the officer assigned to them was male, since the majority of the women said that, at that time, they still felt apprehensive and uncertain when dealing with men. These feelings were particularly intense in the immediate period after leaving the refuge, but were still evident, from time to time, years later. (The issue of women for women services is explored further in Chapter 8.) There was also a profound fear of getting involved with any service that might label them as a bad mother, or, more importantly, have the power to take their children into care.[10] For many of them, this fear had been played upon by their abuser, as a way to control them or to force them to stay or to return to the relationship. And all these fears were magnified by the underlying fear of not knowing who could be trusted and who would be there for them.

These fears and concerns meant that women, especially soon after being rehoused, were extremely reluctant to contact either statutory or any other agencies direct. Directing women to relevant agencies by giving them telephone numbers and contact names and leaving them to make the approach (often described as signposting) was liable to result, at best, in a delay in making contact or no action at all being taken. When they made the initial approach supported by their worker, women said they felt more positive and competent; they felt they were treated very differently, and as a consequence the outcomes were more likely to be productive.[11] As Leanne's experience showed, supporting women in this way, until they gained a degree of confidence, was empowering and showed them how to approach problems and people in a way that achieved the desired result. Jeannie explained how her approach had changed, when she had to deal with a major problem at her younger son's school:

> Before, I used to get angry a lot, quite quick as well, and I've just learnt not to…I'm a lot more calmer. When I asked about that incident last week…normally I would have been going mad – effing and blinding and wanting just to fight with somebody. Do you know what I mean? That's my child and if I think my child's been hurt… And I just see…I don't know, I just see things differently. I've just learnt.

Sorting out problems

It sometimes seemed to the women that pressure from agencies, rather than improving things, was making it more difficult to rebuild their lives. Sally said that:

> It seemed like we were answering to everybody. Asking people for permission. Like being back at home really [with the abuser]. You felt you needed permission to breathe.

'They were all on my back' was a common statement from many of the women, and this was particularly true when several agencies were involved, each dealing with a different aspect of the lives and needs of the family. Often their roles would overlap, and women felt harassed and confused by apparently contradictory demands. It was at times like these that their support worker was particularly valuable in helping them to look realistically at what was being asked of them and how they could best respond. Because the women had begun to trust them, issues that had seemed insurmountable when faced alone could be worked on and the worker could act as a translator, or mediator, between women and agencies. Molly had become confused and frightened by constant visitors, with what she saw as conflicting demands and official letters, to the extent that she felt unable to open any correspondence, in case this created more problems for her. In fact, of course, this tended to make matters worse. As she explained:

I was getting really, really depressed because I'd got Social Services on my back. At the time I'd got, like, the social worker, the family support worker, I'd got a home help thing coming in, the health vis... Everybody was on my back. And it felt like everybody was against me and the only person that was there for me was Lesley [refuge worker]. All the others were slagging me off, saying 'We feel' this, that and the other and all the negative sides. She's putting a positive side [giving me] more incentive to do it.

With Lesley's support, Molly had been able to explain how she felt to the agencies concerned and they were able to talk with her about how they saw their role in helping her and her family. Priorities were agreed with them, so that she and all the agencies and organisations involved were able to work together. As a consequence, she felt less frightened, began to function more effectively and gain confidence, which, in turn, reduced the need for greater agency involvement and enabled the growth of a positive spiral. At the time of our second meeting, fewer agencies were involved and she was continuing to make progress.

With this coordinated effort, attitudes towards agencies could change markedly. Leanne commented that she had changed her opinion of Social Services:

I must admit Social Services have done a lot for me. So my opinion on them has changed a lot. When I first come here, my son was on Child Protection and this, that and t'other. And they soon realised that, once I was out of that situation, I wasn't the problem and they got him off it and I didn't have to see 'em any more...so they did a lot.

Local voluntary services and those run nationally, such as Shelter, were regarded very positively and commended for their attitude, which mirrored that of their support worker. Some of the same fears about making the first approach were apparent – fear of rejection, fear of 'authority' – but once the worker had helped them to make contact, women said they were happy to develop the relationship on their own.

Over the past decade, the issue of domestic violence and abuse has become far more visible. All of the statutory and a majority of other agencies have clear policies and guidelines on dealing with individuals who experience abuse, and have rolled out training programmes for their staff. In talking to workers supporting these and other women, however, it was clear that these policies were not always reflected in the attitude and value systems of the staff who should implement them. Although they could all give examples of individual members of staff who were both understanding and effective in dealing with cases, workers corroborated the views of the women who had encountered dismissive and intimidating behaviour.[12] All too often, they felt, there was a lack of understanding of the devastating physical and emotional effects of abuse, the uncertainty and fears that this had engendered, and the damage caused to feelings of confidence and being in control of their lives. It could be especially difficult to accept that these effects were also present in women who seemed on the surface to be strong and able to cope, but who had, in fact, become accustomed to disguising the nature and extent of the abuse and hiding the effect it had been having on them. Further problems arose when this lack of understanding led to a failure to protect the safety and confidentiality of their details, potentially putting their lives and those of their children at risk.

Refuge workers' perceptions of their role

In each of the refuges involved in this project, I was able to talk to the workers who had supported these women, and I also presented and discussed my findings with workers and managers at a Women's Aid conference in 2007. Enthusiastic and committed, they confirmed the views of women that intensive support during the transition from the refuge to their new home, followed by longer-term support at a lower level, was a key element in the move to independent living and integration into the new community. Supporting women in this way made it less likely that they would return to their abuser because of the problems they faced in the new community.

Placing the needs of the woman and her children at the centre of their work gave focus and shape to the way support was given, with flexibility and 'thinking outside the box' enabling them to work creatively to meet needs. Workers also spoke of the need for sensitivity in knowing when support, encouragement or a more robust approach was appropriate. Practical and emotional support were seen as complementary, with building confidence, self-respect and self-esteem underpinning the more practical aspects of support. As one worker put it:

> You need your emotional support, you need your emotional stability and your self-confidence. You know, the intangibles, to enable you to have the confidence to stay with this new tenancy, or keep that tenancy. I don't know how one thing goes without the other.

The relationship between these two strands of support was not always fully understood by funders, who saw 'signposting' (defined previously) as the way to utilise resources and increase throughput, without considering the mental barriers that held women back from making contact.

From the outset, it was important that women should feel that they were driving the process, making choices, making decisions and gradually moving away from the need for support. This also required workers to set and maintain clear boundaries around what they could and could not do, since they commented that some women could be extremely demanding, expecting everything to be done for them and unwilling to take responsibility for themselves. Success was measured in ways that were not necessarily quantifiable: small changes in appearance and attitude as the work progressed, growth in confidence, and the development of support systems and friendships within the new community. Women who felt secure enough to wave 'goodbye' at an early stage were an added bonus, although workers understood how hard it could be for others to sign off from support.

The work demanded an extensive knowledge base of local information and regulatory requirements, which needed constant updating and retraining if it was to be of use to women, together with the need to build and maintain a network of contacts with other statutory and voluntary organisations. Both of these requirements took time and were more difficult to achieve in rural areas distant from major centres of population, and where scattered communities added to the time taken to travel to and support each woman. All the workers talked of the patchy nature of support provision for women who had experienced domestic violence and abuse, and wanted to see a far more integrated and fully funded support network, so that services were not so stretched and help could be offered to women wherever they were.

This support work was often emotionally draining; workers needed to feel supported and that they could share some of the problems with colleagues. This was easier when there were two or more working in this field, or when they were closely integrated into a refuge and support team. Such an arrangement made it easier to support service users when their prime contact was on holiday, training or unwell, and meant that workers were able to care for themselves as well as those whom they supported.

Families

For many of us, the extended family forms a valuable network to which we can turn for help, advice and, usually, practical and emotional support. Where domestic violence and abuse had impacted on individuals, this support had often been cut off; some had concealed the abuse from their family, partly because of the shame and guilt they felt, but also from a desire to protect them from additional anxiety. Sylvia commented:

> My family would have been there 110 per cent. It was that feeling of 'I don't want to give them something to worry about', you know. My mum developed skin cancer on her arm and my father had had a prostate problem…and there were so many things going off…it was always that feeling 'they really don't need my mess in that mix'. And that is what keeps you in that…unfortunately…that little core of… you know.

Most of the women, as they explained in Chapter 1, had gradually become isolated by the abuser from potential support networks. Gemma, speaking of her second abusive relationship, said:

> He managed to make me not want to talk to my dad, or see my dad, because I didn't want my dad to see the state of my bruises and things like that sometimes. And he'd say 'Oh, why don't you ask your dad to come over', you know, 'your dad's trying to see you.' So I'm thinking, 'Yeah, see me like this? I don't think so.'

When these women first entered the refuge, they had often cut themselves off completely from any remaining contacts with friends and family. The desire to protect those they cared about and keep them safe from the abuser or his/her family (particularly if they were elderly or in poor health) was still in their minds, but this silence was also for their own safety, in case any chance remark led to their whereabouts becoming known. Some of the women had gradually and carefully reduced these precautions while in the refuge, but, once back in the community, they were free to re-establish contact with their families and other friends (and, indeed, their abusers or other former partners and their families) if they wanted to. Contacts were not automatic or obvious choices; families did not fragment along party lines, with allegiance going to one individual or the other. There were supportive members among their partners' families, and hostile and destructive ones among their own, and each of these families might have divided and extended into new relationships. Where they cared for children by a previous partner, he and his family might well come into this complex network of contact. Only one woman was immune from this debate. Having been in care for all her life, Leanne had retained no contacts from the many families and institutions who had cared for her and needed to look for this sort of support elsewhere.

Balancing the need for safety and confidentiality against their desire to rebuild links was crucial, but it was also important for their relationships to be on a new basis; the women knew they had changed and were changing, and they wanted this to be accepted. In particular, they wanted to avoid any contact reminiscent of their experiences of abuse – controlling actions, manipulative behaviour, or being treated as a child. Sylvia's assertion that her family, if they knew, would be there for her '110 per cent' turned out to be fully justified, and this was also true for two of the other women, whose families were there for them, providing emotional support and practical help, without taking over their lives. For three of the others, relationships within the extended family were volatile and constantly changed over the period I knew them. There was always some degree of warm emotional support, but not always from the same individuals. It seemed that this had always been the case and it was almost a ritual that they understood and accepted. Molly, who had also been in care most of her life, but with the same family, whom she regarded as Mum and Dad, explained how she saw it:

> At the moment, we're talking, but we're not talking. At the moment, we're having a bit of a quiet period with them. Yeah, a bit of a quiet period. I do keep in touch with them, you know. It's like proper families. They have arguments, they have disagreements.

The situation was more difficult for the four women where the relationship with their birth families, especially their mothers, might, perhaps, offer a degree of practical support, but where there was emotional distance, and their attempts to reach out did not result in the response they really wanted. This attitude had caused deep sadness, and these women now avoided contact as much as possible, to minimise distress, but felt that the lack of emotional response had left them very much on their own. Lindy had tried, unsuccessfully, to challenge this attitude, but now felt it was better to ignore it:

> My mum's one of these, she's…I'm always there in word, but not actually there in person. She looks as though she's the doting mother, but I've got to be the heap on the floor before she's actually there. I don't see a great deal of them, I don't speak to them very much. I did

confront her once, I said, 'You're only there when I fall to pieces, why aren't you there just to say hello?' And she said, 'I can't believe you said that.' She was quite taken aback. Well, sorry, the truth hurts, but that's how you make me feel.

Others had also decided to cut their losses, but, like Liz, took a more defiant line:

And I thought I'm not even going to let this woman hurt my feelings any more. And so that were that. And until this day I've not spoke to her.

Only from one family had there been a complete lack of understanding and a negative and hostile approach: Briony's mother flatly refused to acknowledge what had happened and insisted on writing to her daughter using her original name, rather than her new identity – a move that could potentially endanger the whole family. Briony had responded by taking avoiding action:

Before she starts belittling me in any way…which she always has done all my life…just to either hang up or pass her on to my kids. So when she phones I always say, 'I'm in the bath' or 'Just nipped over to the shops'. So I avoid talking to her completely.

With the passage of time, there had been illnesses and sudden and unexpected deaths within their families for women to cope with, as well as the loss of ageing parents. Four of the women specifically stressed the difficulties of dealing with yet another loss in their lives. Where other emotional support had been available, they had been able to mourn and move on; for one of them, however, the lack of this support (discussed in Chapter 4) had led directly to the start of a further abusive relationship.

Growth and change

Looking back on their experiences of moving from the refuge and developing, or rebuilding, the basic support systems they needed, women had valued the emotional support they had been given as much as the practical assistance. Once their confidence had begun to grow, they were able to tackle problems more effectively, which, in turn, increased their confidence and self-esteem. To start with, this growing confidence was still quite fragile, but I was able see how the majority of women had gained in confidence over the years. Some were still wary of any 'official' contacts, and they were all aware of circumstances and events that could trigger old patterns of reaction in them – 'pushing my buttons', as Lindy put it. Three women had needed to seek further temporary support from the refuge group; one, when the behaviour of her former partner had caused a crisis in her life; and two, when a new relationship proved to be abusive. A number of women commented that, although they had not needed to contact the refuge for support, the knowledge that, if they did, someone would be there for them and that they would not be rejected, was a thought that had sustained them when difficulties had arisen in their lives.

When we last met, support from the refuge had ceased for all of the women. For ten of them, including Jeannie (who was still technically homeless) other support systems had been established in the background of their lives and were available if necessary. For two women, however, the picture was very different. At the time of our second interview, discussed earlier, Molly had resolved many of her problems and needed less support. She had subsequently suffered life-threatening heart problems, which made it difficult for her to manage on a practical level, including caring for her last remaining child, who had consequently been placed in care. Now on her own, in a reversal of her previous situation, she felt no one was interested in helping her. She had been assessed as not needing practical support, which she was adjusting to, but had also been regarded as not requiring mental support, which she felt she desperately needed:

> But I mean the mental health team came to see me. And then they wrote to me and said that they don't feel that I need any help. And so we're just sitting there thinking 'I do need the help, but you're not prepared to give it me', you know, the counselling and things like that. And with all this, it's all the stress and everything, I'm not supposed to get stressed out, not supposed to get wound up, not supposed to shout and rant and rave, because if I do it'll just kill me. But I do get wound up, I do get stressed out, I do get like…because of not getting the help to get through it.

In complete contrast, Gemma, in temporary housing after fleeing a further abusive relationship, was now involved with many agencies, each dealing with a different issue in her life – physical and mental health, alcohol and drug dependencies, child welfare and protection, and the legal system. Their differing requirements often seemed to her to be in conflict with each other, particularly when appointments with different agencies coincided and each felt they took priority. This apparent lack of joined-up working had left her confused, angry and uncertain as to what she should be doing.

Conclusion

The accounts of the women taking part in this study show clearly the positive impact of providing support both during the process of moving into a new home and for some time afterwards. The relationship with one designated support worker and the emotional aspects of this support – building confidence, self-esteem and self-respect – were as vital to successful outcomes as the provision of practical information and guidance. These 'soft' outcomes are not easily measurable, but without them the 'hard' outcomes – independent living, social integration, a return to employment or education – may not be easily achieved or sustained.

There is a considerable body of research that confirms these findings[13] and supports the need for wider availability of this type of assistance. Providing a high level of support at the time of moving, and sustaining this at a lower level in the longer term, can be seen as cost-effective in that it enables practical problems and mental barriers to success to be dealt with at an early stage, possibly avoiding high-intensity (and expensive) interventions at a later stage. Wider availability of informal contact with refuge groups, self-help and support groups, and local telephone support can also be seen as an effective way of offering practical and emotional support and advice.

There is clearly a delicate balance to be maintained between continuing to offer support and encouraging dependency, since, as workers pointed out, some women will not want to 'let go' – even though they are, in fact, well placed to manage on their own – because of their fears and anxieties resulting from the abuse. It has to be recognised, however, that some service users will always need a degree of support to live independently and contact with a limited number of people whom they will trust to assist them.[14] When this support is no longer appropriate for the refuge services to provide, there is a danger that no other agency will be aware of the need at an early stage, or be prepared to take a lead role where there are multiple problems.

Summary

- There are still major gaps in the provision of services for women experiencing domestic violence and abuse, and a need for a nationwide, fully funded service to provide holistic support.

- Although women gain strength and confidence during their stay in the refuge, the majority require some support during the transitional period and for a while afterwards. The women in this study regarded such support as essential and valued equally the practical help and emotional support they were given.

- A check-back procedure needs to be in place to ensure that women who initially say they do not require support are contacted to reassess the position.

- Support plans and objectives were agreed between the woman and her worker, including risk assessment, safety planning and setting boundaries to the support.

- Women needed to see themselves as active participants in this process and move towards being able to self-advocate. Emotional support that built confidence, self-respect and self-esteem was a key element in this, but workers adopted a challenging approach if this was appropriate.

- Support had to be reliable and consistent to avoid the women feeling revictimised by replicating the unpredictability of the abusive situation. Ideally, it needed to be flexible, tailored to the needs of the family, gradually tapering off as women gained confidence in their own abilities. Although women were aware that this would happen, they felt a sense of loss at the ending and would have welcomed some way of retaining contact.

- Evenings and night times were occasions when women felt particularly isolated and vulnerable and wanted some contact to be available to provide a listening ear.

- They would also have liked low-level support to be available for a longer period for those women that needed it. Some groups facilitate this contact in a variety of ways.

- Although individual agency workers had proved helpful and understanding, women generally held negative views about statutory agencies and were reluctant to approach them directly. Where the approach was made in company with the support worker, outcomes were more likely to be positive and satisfactory.

- Despite major policy initiatives in this area, agencies still needed to become more aware of the specific problems created by the impact of domestic violence and abuse and the effect this may have had on women. More coordinated working would avoid confusion and apparently conflicting requirements for service users.

- Some service users will always need a degree of support to live independently. Where this is no longer appropriate for the refuge services to provide, there is a danger that no other agency will be aware of the need at an early stage or be prepared to take a lead role where there are multiple problems.

- Restoring contact with families could provide valued practical and emotional support, but this was not always the case, and support could be volatile or non-existent.

Notes

1. Coy, Kelly and Foord (2009) found major deficiencies in the provision of specialised services for women experiencing domestic violence in many areas of the UK.

2. This was variously described as resettlement, aftercare, outreach or floating support. 'Outreach' is more often used to describe support work with women and children who are still in the community, and 'resettlement' or 'aftercare' was a more commonly used term. Increasingly, the term 'floating support' is being used to describe both types of service.

3. Safety, as indicated in Chapter 1, was a constant concern for women. Formulating safety plans in advance meant that the whole family knew what to do if problems arose.

4. The term 'advocacy' can be used to describe a number of activities, depending on the context. As it is used here, it refers to the fact that a woman has needs and entitlements from a variety of sources. She may not, for a number of reasons, have the knowledge or confidence to argue her case. In this situation, an advocate works with the woman to remedy this and assist her in receiving a fair hearing.

5. Similar comments were made by newly rehomed and vulnerable individuals in Glasgow to McNaughton (2005).

6. Personal communication, Nicola Harwin, Chief Executive, Women's Aid (2008).

7. Needs also noted by Charles (1994) and McNaughton (2005).

8. Batsleer *et al.* 2002; Hester and Westmarland 2005; Hester with Scott 2000.

9. Hester, Pearson and Harwin with Abrahams 2007; Hester and Westmarland 2005.

10. Lapierre 2008; McGee 2000a; Penhale 2003.

11. Humphreys and Thiara 2002 and Parmar, Sampson and Diamond 2005 report similar findings.

12. Hague *et al.* (2002) found that agency responses to service users had shown some improvements, but that the majority of women felt that they were not listened to, were considered unimportant and their needs were not adequately met.

13. Humphreys and Thiara 2002; Jones *et al.* 2002; McNaughton 2005.

14. Supporting People 2007.

Chapter 4

Community, Friendship
and Beyond

Finding a house, creating a home and accessing support were major steps forward for women in their recovery from the effects of an abusive relationship. Together, these actions began to provide the first two 'building blocks' in their new lives – the means of survival and a sense of safety. And, as a result of these achievements, women had also started to develop feelings of confidence and self-respect. Relating this process to Maslow's ideas of human need (Figure 1.1, page 23), they now needed to build on these foundations by becoming part of the communities in which they lived – accepted by those around them, with friends and acquaintances, and a sense that they belonged there. To reach out in this way was not easy; their past experiences had made them wary of trusting others, fearful of being rejected and suspicious of the motives of those around them. At a much deeper level, connecting to others can also mean being able to give and receive love and being open to the possibility of forming further intimate relationships. This prospect created tension for the women between the desire that many of them expressed for emotional closeness and intimacy and their memories of past love and trust betrayed. Some had been able to resolve this painful dilemma successfully; for others, it had led to further difficulties in their lives.

Part of the community

A sense of belonging within a community will normally include feeling comfortable and at ease in the area in which you live. Women who had been rehoused within twelve miles of their old home, or who were returning to where they were brought up, already had a broad knowledge of the area and its networks to build on, but this was more problematic for those who had moved long distances. Everything was strange – the pace of life, the culture and the environment, even the different words people used. As Liz said, 'I've come a long way, away from everything I know. I don't know a soul. And it's hard.' Not only did they need to become aware of their new neighbourhoods, they needed to relinquish their attachment to the places they had lived in before. This was not a quick and easy activity. Although she had settled into her new home fairly readily, Briony had remained mentally attached to her old area for almost three years before she told me that, at last, there was no yearning to return, however dangerous it might have been.

Research[1] suggests that attachment to a community is facilitated when people feel that they have much in common with those around them, as was now the case for all the women who were in permanent homes. Initially, however, Sally, who had moved between our first and second interviews, had felt lonely on a small, privately built estate, finding her neighbours 'stuck-up'. Having moved to gain more space, she felt far more comfortable in a larger, more diverse community. And Jeannie, whose distant family roots were in Jamaica, had felt 'out of place' in a community that, although ethnically mixed, was largely housed in relatively expensive property. She felt much more at home waiting to be rehoused in a similarly mixed community, but in a less affluent area. Although she was not yet able to make friends from her temporary accommodation, she commented that old friends were far happier to visit in this new environment. Some communities were, inevitably, beginning to change by the time this project was drawing to a close: Charmian wanted eventually to move from an increasingly urbanised environment, and Molly commented that increased turnover was not encouraging community links. Other women, however, had not found substantial changes in their environments.

While they were in the abusive relationship, the women had, either implicitly or explicitly, been deterred from contact with family and friends and, indeed, from any form of social interaction. They were now free to do what they wanted and Leanne told me how much this now meant to her:

> Before I was a bit standoffish and I wouldn't…I didn't like making relationships because my ex didn't like me associating with anybody. But now I can talk to anybody and it's brilliant.

Making this transition was far from easy, and the women were extremely wary of making new friends. Part of their concern was to know how much they could, or should, reveal about themselves, their backgrounds and the abuse they had experienced. While in the refuge, they knew that everyone there had suffered from domestic abuse and that their situation was understood and accepted. But the ingrained habit of pretending to the neighbours in the outside world that everything was fine ('wearing a mask', as Sylvia put it) was hard to overcome. They did not want to appear remote and reserved, but were dubious about how any revelations might be received. Their concerns were echoed by workers, who were aware of the possibility that neighbours could sometimes show a lack of understanding or resentment, perhaps, at a housing allocation that was seen as 'preferential', or share common misconceptions and prejudices about women who experience domestic violence and abuse.

A further issue was the inability to trust others, as a result of the mind games and manipulations practised by their abusers. As Charmian explained, overcoming this took time: 'It's just getting used to who can you trust and who you can't trust. It is a very long process.' In fact, this wariness was still in evidence when we last met. Years after leaving the relationship and with a circle of friends, women recognised that, at base, they really only trusted themselves. Lindy commented, 'I've got a lot of friends. Um...I don't think I'm ever going to totally open up to people.'[2] Not only did women find it hard to trust others, they were also suspicious of the motives behind the smiles. Sylvia, whose parents had given her gym membership in order to encourage her to get out, had, at first, found it hard to recognise that the other women there really wanted to be friendly and were not just being polite. Persevering, despite her initial reluctance to return there, had resulted in a major change in her view of others:

And it's just nice, 'cos you know, you walk in there and it's 'Good morning, Sylvia, how are you?' you know, and you really feel that they genuinely are meaning 'Good morning, Sylvia, how are you?' Whereas I never felt that for quite a long time that...I always felt that, like, it was...that it was a necessity that they said hello rather than they wanted to. But I think that was me. I do now, I didn't then. At the time I was just like 'Just go away', this kind of feeling, you know, curl up and die. But now it's like...it's like being reborn, I suppose, in some ways. It's like learning everything again that I took for granted when I was younger, because I was always a people person, you know, always. ...but it's nice, because if I haven't been for a while...you know how you can tell when people are genuine you know...they'll walk in and they'll go, 'We were so worried about you!' and it's like...it makes me feel good you know that they've actually bothered that they've not seen me, you know. You belong. Yes, that's the word, 'belong', yeah, it's nice.

Support workers were often instrumental in encouraging women to move out of their comfort zones in this way. Liz explained that she had felt nervous, when she started work again, at mixing socially with people whom she saw as above her in the social scale, but her support worker had offered practical advice in a direct and no nonsense way:

> I've got so many different social circles – I've got professional social circles which Daphne [worker] sort of like told me, 'Take the leap.' Daphne were like, 'You get out there, they're only people.'

One interesting development in this process of making friends was the strong bond with their elderly neighbours that had developed for both Leanne and Liz. Leanne had been in care all her life, Liz was not in touch with her birth mother, and for both women, these neighbours had, from the outset, provided stability and emotional support, which was welcomed and reciprocated. Liz described their relationship:

> My next door neighbours … they're in their 60s and they've been my mam and dad for the last seven years. They're there for me through thick and thin. They're so lovely…you know, Mother's day, Father's day, I send them a card and things like that, and vice versa…

With the exception of the two in temporary accommodation (Jeannie and Gemma), all of the women said that they had now built a network of friends within their local communities. For some, it was comparatively small, consisting mainly of neighbours; for others, different and overlapping social circles gave a variety of contacts. Over the years, these growing contacts had increased the women's sense of attachment both to the community around them and to the area they lived in. Briony, for example, had moved from a tentative and rather grudging 'the neighbours are all right, it's quiet enough' to talking enthusiastically about the local amenities, the schools and the parties and places she and her friends went to. Liz, eight years after I first met her, was an enthusiastic member of the community where she had known no one:

> And the people are lovely. They've took me in with open arms. And it's like my colleague, she's actually [born here] and when we're walking down't street I stop and talk to more people than her, and she's like, 'Liz, you've only been here seven years, what's going on?'

When I last met them, Charmian and Molly, although not unhappy where they were, and with local friends, were (as discussed in Chapter 2) hoping, for different reasons, to be rehoused in the future. All of the other women in permanent homes were settled and happy in their new environment, with a circle of friends and every indication that they would be staying there for the foreseeable future. Like most of them, Lindy was clear about the sense of belonging to the place she now lived in and the community around her:

> I love...see I just feel like [it] is home. I come from...when we drive from [the motorway] coming along the road there and you see the hills, the mast...and I just...you know, when you've been a long trip and you sort of 'Ahh ...' – that's how I feel. It's just that view, it's home. It's nice.

Friendships with former residents

During the time they had spent in the refuge, women had valued highly the support of the other residents; they had shared experiences, laughed and cried together and drawn strength from each other.[3] As they left, most had exchanged phone numbers and promised to keep in touch and meet up to continue their friendships. In reality, once they had started to build new networks, these contacts changed radically in frequency and style.

There was no deliberate policy among the Housing Associations, or Local Authorities involved to place women who had experienced domestic violence and abuse in the same neighbourhoods. Although this might have been seen as providing opportunities for mutual support, it might also risk provoking antagonism from the local community[4] or a sense of creating a ghetto. Six of the women had, however, found themselves living in close proximity to a family whom they had known while both were in the refuge. This was not initially seen as problematic, and several had actively welcomed being able to continue their friendship. Unfortunately, all of these relationships had quickly turned sour and unpleasant. Some women had felt that their willingness to help out materially and emotionally was being exploited; sometimes the differing standards of behaviour and discipline in each family had become a flashpoint. Difficulties that had been suppressed during the time in the refuge, in order to make communal living work, became more apparent and less able to be tolerated. For the most part, these difficulties were expressed verbally, but one woman suspected that her neighbour had been responsible for major damage to the exterior of her house, and another had suffered from a malicious phone call to Social Services, accusing her of abusing her children. Obviously, I only heard one side of the story; had I been able to talk to the other protagonists, events might have been described very differently. Nevertheless, it was apparent that although being rehoused nearby, or even in shared accommodation, may be an ideal solution for those women who want it, this is an option that clearly needs very careful consideration. Lindy was not in favour:

> She was in the house opposite me. Which…we were very good friends in the safe house, but it turned quite nasty – all her anger got directed at me. My son got the blame for everything that went wrong, it went awful. And some…I don't know who it was came out…somebody to do with housing…homeless women's stuff…I don't know. My advice now, please don't house people so close to each other…'cos it was closer than that house there.

On the other hand, friendships with former residents where frequency and means of contact could be freely chosen were not extensive, but were highly valued. It was evident that women had thought carefully about who they wanted to remain in contact with and had cut off relationships that they felt might pull them down and make it even more difficult to move forward in their lives. 'I decided to stay away from people that I just didn't get on with,' Liz said. They kept in touch with their chosen associates, using text messages as well as telephone calls, and met up or invited each other home from time to time. This more distant, looser style of friendship seemed very successful and supportive. Three of the women had also instituted this style of relationship with women who were, or had been, refuge support workers. Workers were clear on setting boundaries during a working relationship, seeing clearly the inherent dangers, including the imbalance of power involved and the risk of creating dependency. Here, however, support had ceased a long time previously: two of the workers had retired and they met as equals, but equals who had common ground in their understanding and attitude towards domestic violence and abuse.

Feelings of loss and loneliness

I first met all of these women while they were in refuges, at a time when the concept of forming a new and intimate partnership was the last thing on their minds. Partners who had professed to love them, and whom they had loved, had abused them physically, sexually and emotionally, and their experiences were still raw. Yet many still had feelings of love and loyalty towards their abuser, so that they were confused and unsure of themselves. At the same time, they were struggling with the initial impact of leaving and of all that they had lost in emotional, material and personal terms. The women knew that all of these factors made them vulnerable to pressure to return – either from their partner or from their own mixed feelings – but hoped, like Lindy in Chapter 1, that they would be strong enough to say 'no'.

As time moved on, women were able to think more clearly about their situation and their emotional needs. They remembered the aspects of their relationship that they had valued: the closeness and the good times they had shared and the emotional warmth that had existed, even in an abusive relationship. They grieved over these losses, but the memories of the abuse and its effects were still firmly in their minds. This tension between their experiences of the past and their desire for closeness was hard to resolve; even when they had developed a network of social contacts, there were still, for many of them, deeper feelings of loneliness and isolation that were difficult to deal with.[5] Coupled with this emotional loneliness was a feeling of somehow being incomplete without a partner – another adult to care for and be seen with. Sylvia linked these needs directly with the reasons that she had seen other women returning to the abusive relationship or starting a new one in haste:

> Because I think…and I think even I thought…when you're used to being the other half of somebody, it's like they've died, you know and suddenly you don't know what to do with yourself, you know, because you've always been the person that cooks their tea, the person that washes their clothes, the person that talks to them, does everything with them…and suddenly you haven't got that. And maybe a lot of women, specially some of the ones that I knew that's either gone back with their old partners totally or have jumped straight into various other relationships that have been short-lived, is that they weren't ready in themselves, but hadn't broken that mould and trusted enough that they could be alone.

Sylvia's comments bring into sharp focus the double struggle women faced after leaving the abusive relationship. Not only did they have to rebuild a life that had been demolished by abuse, but they also needed to deal with the emotional impact of the losses they had suffered, including that of a central figure in their lives.

'Different place, same crap'

For two of the women in this study, their need for closeness and caring had led them to start new and ultimately unhelpful relationships soon after leaving the refuge. Looking at their experiences in some detail may offer greater comprehension of why this may happen and what support may help others to recognise and understand their feelings and enable them to renegotiate the terms of any future relationships. Liz had tried to 'rescue' an old friend:

> He were a friend who I knew from up in my old village who had got into a bad way wi't drugs and obviously ended up in prison. So 'cos I were friends, it sort of turned out to be a relationship. So, anyway, he come out of prison and I tried to put him on't straight and narrow… try and encourage him to…you know, he dun't have to always be down there and…build him up sort of thing. Which is not good, 'cos you can't change a person. Because then when I…I moulded him to what I wanted him to be, it weren't enough. And so…and he could never be where I wanted him to be because he just…there's some qualities about him I didn't like and they were just in him. We were fighting constantly and it got nasty.

Her children were unhappy at this new relationship, and Liz herself came to realise that she had changed and was a different person, who was not prepared to put up with abuse again:

> For some reason I'd changed from this person what were quite happy to cower… I mean he were a strong, big built, strong-willed man, and I wouldn't buckle, I were determined not to buckle. And he used to say to me, you know…when things did get physical he said, 'Liz, just…you know, why don't you just shut up?' And I'd be like, 'No, I'm not shutting up, you are not going to shut me up.' And I were more determined this time than I've ever, ever been. I don't know, I were just determined I weren't going to buckle ever again.

This realisation led to an understanding that she was repeating old patterns of behaviour and that things had to change in the relationship:

> I thought, 'Liz, you han't learnt absolutely nothing. When are you going to learn? You can't change somebody.' It's not up to me, I han't got't right to change somebody. Um…and it were that. I thought, 'Here we go again – different place, same crap.' And so I were determined this time just to get shot and stay put.

It was not easy to confront her fears of the past and face this new abuser, but she was able to negotiate an amicable ending and retain his friendship:

> And it's quite weird, actually, because he respects me more for standing up to him afterwards, do you know what I mean. And we

stayed friends even though there were a period where we hated one another. We've actually both learnt summat from experience.

Gemma, whose problems with housing and support were briefly discussed in Chapters 2 and 3, had left her abusive husband and, after a spell in a refuge, had received support to settle in a new community. She suffered a major emotional setback when her mother became seriously ill and subsequently died. Although they had never been close, she had still gone on hoping for some sign of love from her.

> I met Carl on my birthday weekend just before my birthday. Um…I was just so lonely, and I'd just come back from my mum's and she hadn't…it was really upsetting and I went out, I was drinking out 'cos I wanted to make friends. I didn't have anybody in my life. Um…and there he was in a taxi and…I said, 'Ooh, could I share your taxi, are you going anywhere near such and such?' And then I asked him back and, Bob's your uncle, I'd clutched…clatched…you know, sort of fell for him. I was very vulnerable and yeah, he managed to get into my life… our house was a mess and I was a mess. Emotionally very vulnerable. When my mum did die, he was there for me. My mum died in the January, the funeral was the following week. And my family, we just sort of split apart and I…you know, we all fell out and everything, And I had no way of contacting them. And um…it was snowing and it was just a desperate situation. You know, and that was…yeah, that was awful, and Carl had just sort of…I just didn't know anybody. Didn't know where else to turn, anybody I could trust.

Very early on, he began to control Gemma, treating her as his property and using extreme sexual and physical violence towards her:

> It was just like being treated like a piece of meat again. And having no worth and no value to this man. Um…and yeah, I mean he just…I was, because I was so…I wasn't…you know, he didn't even care about me as a human being to kind of keep me safe.

Yet he was also capable of the tender, loving behaviour that she desired so much:

> Because I wanted to keep him…wasn't bothered about anybody else, I wanted that special person. Um, I needed him, I wanted him, specially while Mum was dying. Over time it sort of…it grew and I liked him being around, he did make me laugh and joke, and when things were good they were great. But when they were bad they were awful, and there was no in between.

Periods of happiness, such as happened briefly after their son was born, continued to alternate with episodes of increasing violence, leaving her confused and vulnerable. She broke up with him on numerous occasions, but then asked him to return, feeling that at least it was someone in her life. This lasted for over two years and she resorted to alcohol and using drugs to numb the pain, as she had during her marriage. Eventually, after an episode of extreme violence, she found the courage to give up her home and move right away, recognising that this was essential if she was to stay alive, get her life back on track and, crucially, keep custody of her children. Yet, when I last saw her, she still remembered the tenderness alongside the violence and still had feelings of love and loyalty towards him:

> Despite what he done to me, I still loved him. And um…you know that was a hard thing…you know I just wish he'd loved me back if you like…but he never did, and I had to come to terms with that. I was alone with his son, with my eldest two daughters and another one… his child inside me on the way. And um, we were…as I say, when it was good and he wanted to be loving, I felt so special. Probably because he could make me feel so bad, um, but when he chose to love me, oh, didn't I feel like a princess.

The conflicting emotions that Gemma describes were, as indicated in Chapter 1, common to most of the women who spoke to me, and her comments show clearly the pain and confusion this caused them. At the time of our last meeting, Gemma was receiving treatment and support for her dependencies and she has now attended the Freedom programme,[6] subsequently texting me to say that this was beginning to give her an insight into her own needs and rights in a relationship.

The stories of these two women are not unique. While working with the refuge groups involved with this study, I was able to gather solid evidence on outcomes for eleven of the other women whom I had met previously. These were women where contact was known to be unsafe, their address was not known, or they had chosen not to respond to the letter of invitation. Information about them came primarily from the refuge workers, but was often also mentioned in casual conversation by other women. Three were living independent lives, a further three were in new and apparently non-violent relationships, but two were known to have gone back to their previous relationship, which continued to be abusive, and three had started new and abusive relationships. Some of these women had phoned the refuge for advice; others were in contact informally with outreach workers. From the stories of the women I interviewed and those where there is definite evidence of outcomes, but no contact was able to be made, we know what has happened to 23 women who originally went to refuges after leaving an abusive relationship. Of those women, seven (30%) definitely either started or went back to abusive relationships after leaving the refuge. (There is anecdotal evidence of others doing so, but these could not be confirmed.) This is a deeply disturbing finding and one that is likely to prove costly in terms of its social and economic impact on women and children and in terms of interventions at a later date.

Changing outcomes

From the painfully honest accounts that Liz and Gemma have given, it is possible to see how and why a new abusive relationship may develop and the feelings that can make ending so difficult. It is possible that the other women who have returned to or started new abusive relationships may also be working through a process of leaving and returning, pushed by loneliness and economic difficulties and pulled by the hope that they can make the relationship change or that this time it will be different or that their partner will have changed. This process of leaving and returning, as with Keira in Chapter 1, may ultimately increase a woman's confidence in her ability to manage alone,[7] or, like Liz in this chapter, to recognise that she is repeating old and outworn patterns of behaviour and eventually gain the strength to take a stand against the abuse.

From what women said to me, the emotional loneliness they experienced appeared different from social loneliness and had much to do with their perceptions of themselves as needing another adult in an intimate role within their lives. Sylvia, who identified these feelings earlier, felt that changing self-perceptions was a key element in enabling women to live independently:

> For saying it's [the refuge] one of the worst places you end up, it does centre you to get back out and realise that you do not have to be a victim, you can be strong. You can be alone. And I think that might be one area that I would say could do with enforcing slightly. Maybe on the very end of leaving…and on the very early outreach. You know, getting through to somebody that you can be alone, you don't need to fall apart. Nothing bad's going to happen. You know you can live alone, you don't need somebody else.

In the stress, excitement and anxiety that women described at the time of moving out, it seems likely that any additional information like this might well be forgotten, but the value of providing emotional support of this nature has been shown to be of immense significance in helping women to move on with their lives. Drop-in sessions, self-help and support groups have already been mentioned as a means of offering support and countering general feelings of loneliness and isolation, but Hester and Westmarland (2005) also found that support groups and structured groupwork programmes were valuable in helping to change women's perceptions of themselves, enabling them to see themselves as individuals who were in control of their lives and as worthy of respect by those around them. Evaluation of a number of these groups reached similar conclusions, with women reporting that they had gained inner strength and confidence in their ability to manage on their own.[8] Many of the women interviewed for these evaluations stressed that, as a result of these courses, they now demanded mutual respect in any future relationships, including those at work or in the home. They commented, however, that these courses, although life-changing, were intense, and that it could be difficult to absorb the information and assimilate what they had learnt into their daily lives, particularly in view of all the other new tasks they were undertaking. Some had been able to attend courses more than once; others had benefited from the availability of informal support groups where they could support each other as they learnt and practised new ways of being, enabling them to get the best out of what was on offer.

Although the majority of the women in this study had clearly been able to develop insight and understanding without additional support of this nature, others may benefit from the additional impetus given by groups and structured courses. It would seem, therefore, that making courses of this nature readily available to those women who wanted them soon after resettlement would be of benefit in increasing self-awareness and understanding, enabling women to make balanced judgements before starting or returning to a relationship. Facilitating the formation of support groups run by women themselves would also be a valuable adjunct to these programmes.

Finding their own pathways

None of the other women had returned to their partners or started a further abusive relationship. Several agreed with Jeannie that 'it would be like putting an old noose round my neck!' Five of them were currently

COMMUNITY, FRIENDSHIP AND BEYOND / 81

living independently with some, or all, of their children and, although not altogether ruling out the possibility of forming a new relationship, there was a general feeling that this was unlikely at present. Should the right individual come along, however, it was clear that matters would be on a very different footing from before, as Briony explained:

> I like the fact that if I want to go out, I go out. And if I don't want to go out, I won't. If I want to cook, I will, if I don't, I won't. So I like the fact that I've got my own freedom of choice to do what I want to do and not have to worry what the consequences are going to be. So…I like that. I've been doing it now for a few years. So…God help any bloke that tries to stop me doing it again. It'd be nice if one came along. Even just for the little cuddles and things like that. You miss those, but…no, I'm quite happy. Got nobody's shirts to iron, nobody's, you know, dirty underwear to wash, apart from my own and the kids'. I like the fact…I like being independent now.

Although Charmian was also living independently, she was tentatively resuming a friendship with a former boyfriend who had been abused by his wife. As she explained, this was a delicate process for both of them:

> He has been through it. He's been through the mill. We've got a lot in common. [I'm] not exactly nervous, it's just…I can't put my finger on it. But, I mean, I like him and he likes me. But it's just getting to know each other again. I'm not in a rush. So we'll just take it bit by bit. You know, there's a lot of regrets that you would like to put right, but you just can't do it, you've just got to get on with what's…

Leanne had found a new partner, but was adamant that she would never again want a live-in relationship:

> I'm a lot stronger than I ever was. And I wouldn't let anyone treat me like that again. No way! No, I wouldn't live together with somebody again, I don't think. I'm happy on my own, it's on my terms. And if I want her to go, she goes. I mean I'm not going to kick her out or owt, but I mean I choose when I see her. And it suits me and it suits Nigel [son] and we still get that time on our own.

An added bonus for Leanne was the way her new partner's family and friends had welcomed her and her son into their lives, and this had given her the close family relationships that she had never known before. This welcome from a partner's family had also happened for Sally, whose own family relationships were extremely volatile. She was now living with the father of her eldest daughter, and although he had a previous conviction for violence towards another woman, both were aware that violence was not an option in their renewed relationship:

> 'Cos he know he's...I've told him and his mum and sisters told him, if he gets in any more trouble, then he loses us. Because we're not going through what we went through again. He says, 'I never want to lose you again.'

Molly had also got back in touch with an old boyfriend, who was now a regular visitor. Both he and his daughter were helping to care for her, but she was well aware that her frustration at her failing health and increased medication led to her being physically and verbally violent towards him. Although fearful that she might drive him away, she felt unable to alter her behaviour.

At the other end of the spectrum were Lindy and Liz, who were both now in non-violent, long-term relationships and were planning to get married the following year. They spoke frankly and movingly about the fears that they had had to face in learning to trust again, lowering their defences and believing that they could have a loving and caring partner. Liz, after having had one false start, had struggled to show her softer side:

> I have found it hard meeting somebody that's actually loving and tactile and...he's got such a heart of gold. I found it at first quite stifling that he loves me 100 per cent and he...you know, he finds me physically attractive, and all them things, you know, with compliments. I found it a bit hard to get used to and I found it a bit suffocating so we... obviously boundaries went up on my end. But he's stuck in there and I'm starting to soften to it now and see that he han't got a game plan, he's not manipulative, and he truly really loves me for me and...and so that's nice, it's a nice feeling to feel that comfortable and...takes a lot of stress away actually, you know, that you have to be guarded and always thinking what are they after and things like that. It's all them thoughts have gone and it's quite nice to just be content. So yeah, that's nice.

Both men were very different from their previous partners and this, too, had presented problems. Lindy had needed encouragement from her support worker to help her to take the risk of developing the friendship:

> He's completely different from what I usually go for. And when I first met him I found it very difficult to bond with him because he was what I'd call a nice man. Completely different from what I'd go for. And I

sort of had a chat with the social... She said, 'Lindy, I will give you training,' because women always apparently go for the same sort of people. Yeah. And we had a chat and I thought, 'Right I'm going to give him a chance.' Very dubious and I thought, 'Ooh no, I don't think he's the one for me,' but... He's fantastic. He's just turned into everything I've always ever wanted. He's caring and loving and considerate and... we talk and talk. I mean, he knows everything about me. He's met me through this and knows all about it, and it's not put him off.

Here, too, the question of what to reveal and what to say to the new family was also a hurdle to be overcome:

When it come to meeting his parents, I still do sort of beat myself up about it... I said to him, 'Please do not tell them anything about me.' He said, 'Why?' I says, 'Well, how would you like if your daughter came home to say...' – you know – 'your son came home to say, "Mum, I've met this lovely woman, she's homeless, she's got three children from two different fathers, she's been married twice and he beat the living daylights out of her, and she doesn't work, she's got no money"?' I said, 'Would you be impressed?' I says. So the badge I've got for me, I'm not impressed with my badge. But I met them, and then they found out, and I think, even to this day, I don't think I'm good enough for them, but there you go.

Even with their new-found happiness, fears crept in from time to time; memories of the past made them wary of fully trusting the strength of the relationship and of believing that their happiness was genuine and that they could accept it. Lindy knew that this reaction could affect her relationship with her new partner, but found it difficult to accept in her heart that things were different:

I'll always have is...I'm always expecting...that's my relationship with John, I'm waiting for that...it's like...do you know if you go out and you're having a nice evening, having a few drinks and...I'm waiting for that nastiness to turn still and I'm thinking, 'He's not Damien, but he just...' – you do sort of go backwards and forwards through time. But it's um...as I say, John's always saying, 'Lindy, please, I'm not Damien.' 'I know you're not, but it's real.' You're waiting for it to happen and it's not happened, so why am I waiting? I don't know. Contradicting myself now, aren't I?

These feelings of wariness – the difficulty of trusting others and the fear that things might go wrong at any time – were common to all of the women and show, yet again, the way abuse had infected their lives.

Because of these fears, settling into a new community and making friends and acquaintances was not an easy process, but it was essential if they were to combat loneliness and isolation and develop a new and satisfying life. Taking risks and reaching out had paid off for the majority of them; being accepted and appreciated had taught them to value themselves. They were exploring new links and emotional relationships, but, at the same time, needed to wrestle with the practical problems of independent living.

Summary

- Establishing a home and accessing support were major steps forward for women. They now needed to connect to the community around them and make friends.

- While in the abusive relationship, women had been isolated from social contact. They were now able to build new friendships, but were intensely wary of doing so, fearing rejection, unsure as to whom they could trust and suspicious of the motives of others. As time went on, these fears grew less, and most women had established a network of acquaintances. They felt at home in their communities and had a sense of belonging there.

- Women who had been rehoused in close proximity to families they had known in the refuge had initially welcomed this, but differences, which had been tolerated while in the refuge, had eventually caused these relationships to break down. In contrast, friendships where frequency and means of contact could be freely chosen were valued and carefully maintained.

- Of the women where outcomes were known, at least 30 per cent had either returned to or started new abusive relationships soon after leaving the refuge, with emotional loneliness and isolation seeming to play a key role in this process. This is a deeply disturbing finding. It is possible that these women may be following a pattern of leaving and returning to abusive relationships and that, as some in this study have done, they may gradually develop the confidence to take a stand against the abuse.

- Forming new, intimate partnerships was a difficult area for women to negotiate. They missed the closeness and warmth present even in an abusive relationship, but feared to commit themselves to a relationship that might mirror past experience. Although most were living independently, a few had renewed previous non-violent partnerships and others had found new, non-violent partners. For all of them, it was difficult to trust and reveal their feelings and there was always an element of uncertainty in their approach.

• Support and self-help groups and structured groupwork programmes offer help to women in changing their perceptions of themselves and developing confidence in their own abilities. Although not an easy option, they are highly regarded by the women who attend them and may be a way of assisting women to recognise that they are capable of living independently and to renegotiate the terms of present and future relationships.

Notes

1. Livingston, Bailey and Kearns 2008. Further positive attachment indicators noted in this research included living in an area for longer and building good social networks.

2. The British Crime Survey 2006–7 (analysed in Povey *et al.* 2008) reported that 15 per cent of women who experienced abuse stopped trusting people and had difficulties in making other relationships.

3. Abrahams 2007; Kirkwood 1993.

4. Charles 1994.

5. Poignantly expressed to Malos and Hague by a woman who confessed, 'You are very lonely in your heart' (1997, p. 405). Researchers have consistently recorded the influence of loneliness and isolation in influencing women, particularly soon after leaving the refuge, in returning to an abusive relationship or starting new and unhelpful relationships prematurely (Binney *et al.* 1981; Charles 1994; Humphreys and Thiara 2002).

6. The Freedom programme, available in many locations across the UK, aims to help women to recognise abuse and to gain the self-esteem and confidence to meet their own needs and improve the quality of their lives (Craven 2000).

7. This pattern has been noted in other research (Batsleer *et al.* 2002; Dobash and Dobash 1979; Kirkwood 1993).

8. Barns with Abrahams 2008; Batsleer *et al.* 2002; CordisBright Consulting Ltd 2006; McTiernan and Taragon 2004.

Chapter 5

Managing a New Life

Life with a controlling partner had severely limited the women's ability to organise and manage their own lives and to take decisions on family matters. The constant threat of physical, emotional or sexual violence meant that all their actions and activities had been carried out with an eye to what their partner's reactions might be and the consequences for themselves and their children. Now that they had moved back into the community, women were free to plan their daily lives without these constraints, to take control and establish order and predictability instead of chaos. This was not an easy process, however; it felt quite lonely and a heavy responsibility to take all the decisions that would shape the family's lives now and in the future. The lack of confidence in themselves and their abilities, which had resulted from the abuse, initially meant a lot of anxious internal debate on what they should be doing and what were the best options.

Money (or the lack of it) was a key area of concern for most of them; it limited what they could provide for their children, restricted their access to training and employment, and made it difficult for the family to engage in social activities such as holidays and excursions. For some, debts incurred during the relationship, or after moving out, were an added burden, and underlying all these concerns was the issue of continuing safety for themselves and their children. But as they began to settle in to their new lives, looking to the future became more of a possibility, although this was limited by their lack of resources.

Counting the pennies

When I first met these women, all twelve were in receipt of some form of state benefit. All had worked at some stage of their lives, but six had not done so for a considerable time, either because of family responsibilities or because their partner had prohibited it. The other women had been in paid employment at the time of leaving the relationship, but had had to give this up when they came to the refuge.[1] At the time of our last discussions, four of those who had previously worked were again in employment – one in a low-paid job, one back with her previous employer, and two, after early struggles, were now professionally qualified and in full-time work. The remainder, two of whom were now registered as disabled, continued to receive state benefits.

During their stay in the refuge, the women paid weekly fixed charges for their accommodation and services, with the rest of their income available for food, clothing and any other necessities. Once they had moved out, this simple arrangement ceased and they needed to budget for the different bills they would receive, including allowing for the utility and services bills, which came in throughout the year. Obviously, the need to keep themselves and their children fed and clothed was their first priority, but, as discussed in Chapter 2, they also wanted to create a comfortable home, with their own choice of furniture and decoration. Meeting all these demands, for those on benefits or a low income, meeting all these demands required immense skill and a determined and disciplined approach to daily life.[2] Briony was typical:

> I do everything on a weekly basis. Go to the post, pay all the bills every week. And then whatever's left, fair enough. Go and do the shopping. Then I'll get my tobacco. And then, if there's any left, they get sweets and things. Which suits me. So I'm usually skint… I get my money and I'm skint like but…they get their treats and things like that. But I like to know where I'm at. 'Cos money doesn't go very far. Not with three hungry kids.

This delicate balance could easily be upset by sudden and unexpected demands – for example, the need to repair or replace an essential piece of household equipment, or increases in the cost of utility and council charges. This financial uncertainty and the continued need for frugality was a constant strain on the women, resulting in them, as they said, 'feeling down'. For those who remained on benefits, this situation was unlikely to change. A study by the Joseph Rowntree Foundation in 2009 showed that people of working age on benefits are still below what is generally considered to be a minimum income for an acceptable standard of living.

Food was a particular source of anxiety. All of them were very much aware of what constituted a healthy diet and talked of how important this was for their children's health, but they were concerned that financial pressures made it extremely difficult to provide as they would have liked. Many of them talked of the efforts they made to do this: spending considerable amounts of time hunting for bargains in the food line, accessing cheaper shops and taking advantage of local markets. Careful budgeting meant that they could then provide a bit extra for special occasions, such as birthdays or Christmas.

A further drain on the budget was the need to provide clothing and equipment for their growing children. Even though they knew their children understood the situation, they felt frustrated and unhappy that they could not afford to buy the sort of clothes and equipment that would put their children on equal terms with their peers.[3] Jeannie felt this lack was particularly hard on her eldest son:

> They're still clothed decently. I haven't got everything that...you know... the latest...specially Kyle, 'cos he's big now, he wants the trainers and that and this. Do you know what I mean? But he understands.

Managing debt

This tight control of money and expenditure had frequently come through bitter experiences in the past. Leanne was determined not to give way to the euphoria of having money to spare:

> It was like 'I've got all this money'. I thought 'No'. As soon as I get my bills in, I pay 'em. I've messed up so many times before in the past and I have been in debt and getting loans to pay loans...interest on debts...

For five of them, struggling to repay debt was an added burden on their resources. Sylvia and Sally were repaying debts that had been incurred during the abusive relationship, as a result of their partner's actions. The other three had run into debt after leaving the refuge. Jeannie had not clearly understood her responsibilities under the housing system, and Molly, as discussed in Chapter 3, had become overwhelmed by her situation and had ignored warning letters. Briony had taken out a small loan to enable her to take her three children abroad on their first ever holiday. This had been so memorable for all of them that she had done the same thing the following year. Repayment costs had mounted, however, and she was now cutting back drastically on other expenditure to get clear of debt as soon as realistically possible. One thing, however, which she said she had learnt from her present difficulties, was that it was far better to bring matters into the open, talk about her finances and negotiate about payment, rather than letting things mount up.

When money was being deducted from income before they received it (as in the case of rent arrears), the women had little or no control over the process or how long it would take before they would be out of debt. Sally had calculated that, by the time this happened, she would be 103! Those women who had some control over their finances showed me detailed calculations as to when they would be debt free, down to the month and the year, but always with the realistic comment that this depended entirely on there being no further emergency. To maintain this strict regime, often for several years, was not easy. Sylvia said:

> Well, I mean, I get £97 a week, so it's under £400 a month. Well, the two loans that was from when we were a couple is £202.20 [repayments each month]. That's over two weeks' money in that alone. So in the other two weeks' money I have to feed us for a month, petrol for a month, gas and electric, water rates, and all the other bits and bobs you need in the house, you know, toiletries, sanitary wear, clothing, shoes, petrol, cigarettes. I mean…I'll be buggered if I give up my cigarettes because it's the only luxury I have – and I mean I only have about three packs a week as it is, you know. But the bugbear of it is like when you think you've got all that and then you've got to add £45 rent and £800 a year poll tax [in fact, council tax] on top of that.

In some instances, support workers had been able to help them in starting to solve their problems, and two of the women commented on the advice and assistance they had been given by voluntary debt counselling agencies (although it was not always easy to follow their advice in the reality of daily living). Looking at the whole situation of planning and managing their money after leaving the refuge, many of the women felt that it would have been helpful to have had specific life skills training in this area and others linked to it, such as applications for grants, before moving to their new homes.[4] This would have been especially helpful for those women who, during the period of the abusive relationship, had not been allowed to handle financial matters. One or two suggested that, if it had been possible to do this while they were still in the refuge, this would have eased the task of the support worker.

The costs of working

Employment has traditionally been seen as the route out of poverty, and government policy has been designed with the aim of assisting this transition.[5] All of the women I talked to agreed with this concept in principle. Like Jeannie in Chapter 1, they saw work as offering them dignity, respect and a long-term future.[6] In reality, however, the situation they faced was not straightforward, as several complex factors affected their ability to seek and retain work. The first was the situation that is frequently referred to as the poverty or benefits trap, whereby obtaining paid work means not simply the cessation of direct benefit income, but also the loss of other financial and associated benefits linked to this entitlement. Although this might, depending on circumstances, be offset by tax credits, there were major additional costs associated with returning to work – suitable clothing, transport and childcare. If women had no qualifications or special skills, as was mainly the case, they were unlikely to find a job well paid enough to compensate for their increased outgoings, particularly if they were looking for part-time work to fit in with the needs of their children.[7] Their families were also a factor in the location of a possible workplace, since women felt it was important, as the only adult, to be fully involved with their children's schools and easily reached if problems arose. They therefore needed jobs that were flexible enough and local enough to facilitate this involvement.

Women received mixed messages from the support agencies they dealt with: some tried to encourage them into work, while at the same time others advised the same women not to look for work, so that they could continue to receive income support. Sylvia was somewhat surprised:

> I've never been into a Jobcentre where they tell you not to work…but I have now! They put my calculations in, they looked at my outgoings, and…I'm actually something like £14.50 under the poverty line. And going back to work with having to find rent and poll [council] tax and everything, they said you just couldn't do it at the moment, you just viably would not be able…you would be worse off. And I'm like 'Eh?' She says, 'Well, either that, or you'd need a job that paid £9.50 an hour to live how you're living now, to pay your debts.' Honestly, my face must have been a picture because I just sat there with my mouth hanging open, you know, saying 'Pardon?' They said, 'Perhaps we'll look at it in six months, but at the moment, no, we don't think it looks viable for you to work.'

As well as these financial dilemmas, there were major considerations around their children, who had witnessed the violence and sometimes suffered alongside their mothers. After the major upheavals and emotional stress that they had endured, mothers were concerned to provide a stable home environment to aid the recovery of the family as a whole. With so many changes having taken place in so short a time, they needed to feel sure that their children would be able to cope with a further change in their situation if their mothers went out to work. For some children, this was a longer process than for others, even within the same family. Several years after leaving the relationship, Sylvia was still unsure of how her young son would react:

> Making sure Daniel was happy and settled and centred again was a big kind of thing that I wanted to work on once we'd got our own environment. I would have liked to have gone back to work earlier. But I just really haven't felt that Daniel is centred enough for me to work full time going off to… I think he'd lost enough in his life, you know, and he got very kind of clingy. And I thought he really isn't ready to be said, 'Oh, you've got to get up 7 o'clock to go to a stranger and you're going to be there till 6 o'clock to a stranger as well.' I think he needed…with everything changing, you know going from having everything…

Once mothers were reasonably satisfied on this point, they had to tackle the problem of finding childcare that was affordable and of good quality; it was vital that children did not experience any further emotional damage. Flexibility was also an important requirement, particularly where women had children who were at different stages of educational development and might be in schools a distance apart. The availability of supervised activities and clubs, after school and during the holidays, also came into the picture, if mothers were to be able to take up full-time employment. Many schools are now setting up such schemes, but they are by no means universal and are heavily resource-intensive. Although there has been an increase in the number of childcare centres available, these were often not local to where the women lived; and, as Jeannie pointed out to me, places offering free, or subsidised, places (usually run by the local council) had long waiting lists, and private schemes were prohibitively expensive. And even subsidised places were likely to be beyond their means.

Gaining qualifications

Going back into vocational training or education and gaining qualifications would seem the obvious way to improve the chances of a better-paid job and overcoming the benefit/wages trap. But here, too, there were difficulties to be overcome. Although some colleges run short, free, taster courses, and there are community centres that provide basic training, gaining higher qualifications generally requires going to a recognised centre for further education. Even when subsidised, as it can be for those on benefits, this is not cheap, particularly on an already overstretched budget. And for courses where student loans and grants are available, there is the commitment to repay what can amount to a sizeable debt on becoming qualified. Liz, who had opted for this route to permanent employment, explained:

> My intention were to do my DipSW (Diploma in Social Work) and at the time when I did the HND (Higher National Diploma), the DipSW were an added year top-up. But then in my second year of HND they changed it to where DipSW was a three-year course in itself. I didn't want to do another three years at college. ... To me it were a big fat waste of time and finances, because obviously I had to have student loans and student grants and be paying...I still pay 'em off now out of my wage, you know, a big expense for nothing, really, I see that as.

Childcare was part of the considerations here as well; although some colleges provided low-cost or free crèche facilities, these were designed for younger children, and if women had to make their own arrangements, they ran into the same problems as if they were seeking work.

No way forward

For six of the women, any possibility of improvement in their situation seemed a long way off. Molly was now too ill to work, although she had, before that, begun to gain basic National Vocational Qualifications (NVQs) at a local community centre that provided free crèche facilities, and had hoped to take this further. Maddy, whose adolescent children could be left on their own, had also started to improve her basic skills at a local centre, but had given up when she felt patronised by her tutors and unsettled by the constant changes in staff. Assessed as incapacitated for work, she was now acting as an informal carer for her new grandson. Of the two women in temporary accommodation, Gemma needed to solve her substance dependencies and personal difficulties before any form of work could be considered, although she wanted, eventually, to move into social work, having understood the difference well-trained social workers could make. Jeannie, however, had taken a couple of short, free, taster courses at the college close to her temporary accommodation, which fitted around her children's school times, and this had rekindled her desire to go back to studying when she was in permanent housing, ultimately aiming for a job in the health and social care field. Again, however, this would depend on the cost of the courses and the availability of acceptable childcare.

Lack of access to affordable childcare locally was also cited as a problem by Briony and Sally, who had children well below the age at which they could legally be left on their own. Briony felt that she would be able to look for work once the eldest was over this age, but only providing the financial equation worked out. Sally was uncertain if this would be possible, since she felt that both of her children had been very badly affected by the abuse (discussed in Chapter 7). One child had been assessed as having special needs and she was also now caring for the children of her partner, one of whom had similar problems. She felt that, for some time to come, they needed her to be at home for them.

Pathways into work

Volunteering can provide not only social contact and work experience, but may also offer a pathway into paid employment. Sylvia, having received debt counselling for herself, was now working as a volunteer in the same agency, gaining the knowledge and skills and working for the qualifications that she hoped would enable her to get a job in this field. She was able to fit this around her son's school activities, thus avoiding the need for childcare. Interestingly, her greatest difficulty at work was the uncertainty and self-doubt caused by abuse, which made her query her own decisions, a problem that may well be a deterrent to other women in seeking employment:

> This is a game, the slight knock on things that I haven't quite shaken over the years of second guessing, still…not trusting myself that first time around. And I think that's the thing that I notice more, how it's affected me, is just always this second guessing, always thinking, like, 'Well, am I sure about that person? Am I sure about what I'm saying?' Whereas before it's, like, I was totally confident. You know, I was always a confident person especially in a work-ethic environment. And now it's always that little bit 'Ooh, I'm not so sure'. Whether it's just 'cos I've been out of work and haven't got that motivation or feeling going or what, I don't know. So that is something that annoys me inside, you know. I'm thinking is it age, is it because you were so wrong then that you're so scared now of being wrong again, you know.

Charmian was attending a local college close to her son's school and with the same hours. She had already gained GCSEs in English, Maths and Computer Skills, aiming, eventually, to gain a job as a bookkeeper, although she was concerned that her age would be against her by the time she had finished her studies. Studying had given her immense pleasure and a sense of achievement, but this had come only at a personal cost, not only in economic terms, but in the limitations it had placed on other aspects of her life.

The four women who were now in paid employment had all taken very different routes in returning to work and in dealing with the associated challenges of finance and childcare. Keira had confided in the human resource division of her large firm before going to a refuge, and arrangements had been put in place to enable her to return to the firm, once she had settled in her new home. Her children were old enough to be left on their own, and she was confident that they were mature enough to be able to deal with her absence. She told me that returning to work had been a big factor in her recovery, because of the sense of normality it had given her:

> I knew exactly who I was and what I was, and what I needed to get back on track, and that was to go back to work. Because that was a big part of me. And once I did that everything else seemed to fit into place quite well. I'm making it sound easy; it wasn't – it was very damned difficult.

Leanne worked as a cleaner, combining a number of jobs to provide a basic income. She had been able to work hours that fitted around her son's school and activities, increasing her hours as he grew older and more settled. She expected to be working full time within the next few months. The work suited her and she didn't see herself doing anything else:

> See, I'm not very good reading, writing, that way. I like cleaning, I enjoy it, it's quite good money, so I'll probably clean till I can't do it no longer. I think that's it – once you get into that, cleaning, you get stuck in a rut.

At the time of leaving the refuge, both Liz and Lindy had families in which the children were older and siblings were happy to keep an eye on the younger ones. This made a considerable difference to their ability to seek work or gain qualifications. Liz had started off in the same way as Sylvia, by volunteering in social care agencies, before finding paid employment in this field. At the same time, she started a grant-aided qualification, which had led to a full-time job and subsequent progression. On leaving the refuge, Lindy had found a full-time job in a care home, while studying in the evenings. Unfortunately, an attack from a resident had brought back all her memories of abuse and resulted in a period of sick leave. She returned to work in a slightly different area of social care, gained an NVQ at level 3, and had now taken on extra responsibilities. Both women would have liked to take their training further, but had been deterred by the cost and the probability of long-term debt. They saw their qualifications not simply as a pathway to a better job, but as proof that they were respected and worthy members of society and capable of achieving success.

It was very noticeable, over the years I had known these women, that they had gained in confidence and that their achievements had changed their views of themselves and their place in the world. For Lindy, in particular, who, at our first meeting, had been suicidal and saw herself 'at the bottom of the heap', life had completely changed:

> I think I sat down in the past and go to myself, 'I'll show you all.' At work I…well, I sat in a conference the other day…and there's me and the social worker and the community nurse and…no, I'm very… it's nice. I feel important. Yeah, yeah, I quite like it. I'm quite…quite a few people I've met throughout…since I've been [here] said, 'You ooze confidence.'

It is clear, from the stories of the women who are currently working and those who are studying as a way into work that their achievements have boosted their confidence and self-esteem, in addition to any financial rewards. None of them would say that this had been an easy path to take; although they had older children or were able to work around school hours, financial and time constraints had considerably restricted their lives, and they needed immense determination and dedication to overcome the difficulties they faced.

Research has shown that although the majority of women do want to enter employment, they feel frustrated and held back by the economic and social barriers they face.[8] The limitations and contradictions around employment and education, which were discussed earlier, seemed constantly to erect barriers against moving forward, making it difficult for women to see the possibility of improving their situation. With the loss of confidence and self-esteem resulting from the abuse, there is a danger, as Leanne commented, of becoming 'stuck in a rut'. The additional support and payment measures proposed by the government are designed to assist the move back to paid work or training and education, and may help to change this. If these measures are to succeed, however, there are aspects that need to be addressed more fully: childcare that is accessible, affordable, of good quality and responsive to the needs of families; the cost of training and education; and the whole situation regarding basic income structure.[9] Together, these present major drawbacks to women seeking to re-enter the workforce. Additionally, there needs to be a greater understanding, on the part of agencies and organisations, of the longer-term effects of domestic violence and abuse on women and children and their implications in terms of employment.

Taking a break

For most families, taking the children out for the day, going out with friends and having a holiday together are important aspects of their lives, but occasions that most of us tend to take for granted. Many of these women had never been allowed to enjoy this freedom and they were eager to see new places and give their children the same opportunities as their peers. Where finances permitted, this had become a real pleasure, but, for those on low incomes, to do so was a struggle. As they pointed out, the majority of attractions designed for families are expensive in any case; apart from the initial entry fee, there were likely to be internal charges for rides, guides and food. These mounted up exponentially with the numbers of children and as they grew, especially where there was more than one child of school age. Briony joked with her children that drastic measures might become necessary:

> 'Cos I took the kids out yesterday. It was 40 quid on nothing. It was a waste of time, complete and utter waste of time. Uh...but, and there's another thing coming up in a couple of weeks or so's time. So I want to take them there. For that we're going to need £80 to £90. You've got to pay to get in, like £2 each. Except for Jamie – I won't have to pay for him. 'Cos it's a metre...under a metre they get in for free. But both the girls are over a metre. I told Ellie that I would chop her off at the knees!

For this particular family, one precious source of pleasure had been regained: after being rehoused, the family dog had come home. Only a puppy when they left, a pet fostering scheme had cared for her for over a year, until they could be reunited. Other women who lived in localities where these schemes did not operate had been forced to leave much-loved pets behind or give them away.

As with other aspects of life on a low income, women felt guilty that they were depriving their family of the things that other children enjoyed.[10] They worked hard to find things to do that were both interesting and inexpensive, such as going swimming together, to parks or on walks in the country. Often the children were involved in budgeting household expenditure, having their say in where the money went and understanding some of the problems.

Holidays were another area where ingenuity and resourcefulness had been employed to give mothers and children the opportunity to relax together at low cost. For some families, staying in caravans and camping had proved relatively cheap and enjoyable; for others, adult children living away from home or other members of the extended family had generously stepped in to provide holidays for mother and children, or had taken children away with their own families. Sometimes, these had proved to be the trip of a lifetime: Sylvia's brother had cashed in seven years of Airmiles to bring her and her son to America; Jeannie's cousin and aunts had clubbed together to take her eldest son to visit family in Canada and the United States.

Other women had been able to access free holidays nearer home. Charmian had experienced acute stress soon after moving from the refuge, partly because of the effects the abuse had had on her young son. Her Family Social Worker (FSW) had been able to find a holiday to give them all a short break:

> I mean, I were cracking up, because I didn't think I'd be able to get through it. I got a Family Funding holiday for me and my kids. And we went to Butlins at Skegness for a week. And it was absolutely wonderful. 'Cos we hadn't had an hol- … I hadn't had an holiday since the '80s. So Jenny [FSW] says, 'Right, I'll put your name down and see if we can get you one.' And we ended up going into a caravan at Skegness at Butlins. So we absolutely loved it.

This experience had been so successful and worked for all the family that she had made this a priority in her budgeting for future years. Yet this pleasure, coupled with her commitment to studying and a low income, came at a price:

> Time for me? I don't have time for me. I don't go out, I don't have a social life, I don't do anything. I just go to college, save my money and then enjoy taking t'kids away somewhere. So I don't go out. I don't drink, you know. Practically in these four walls of a night. Don't go anywhere. I'm in bed by nine. It is hard, yeah. But…um…I wouldn't want to go into town anyway. But even if I could go somewhere like to pictures or summat, I couldn't take Andrew, because he's not old enough. There's nobody to babysit, my mum don't want to know. So

I'm just stuck on my own with him. Which I've had to cope with ever since he were born really.

As her comments show, poverty also breeds isolation from other forms of social life. Paying for babysitters was beyond the budget of these women, and where children were too young to be left on their own, or when there was no adult or older sibling willing to keep an eye on them, women were restricted from taking any time out for themselves as individuals. Dearly though they loved their children, several of them commented that, just occasionally, they would have liked 'me' time in their lives. Lindy emphasised the importance of keeping a space for herself if she was to be able to care for her children and manage the challenges of their new lives:

If I don't look after me, no one's getting anything. No, the children still do come first, but I sometimes get a bit selfish and say, 'No, it's my time, go away', but I do it. Yeah. You've got to. If you don't, you're just going to end up…you've got to class yourself first.

Where children were older, or appropriate care was available, this additional freedom to relax, make friends and take small, inexpensive trips out, without lengthy interrogation and criticism on return, was exhilarating, boosted confidence, extended social networks and helped to rebuild social skills.[11]

Safety

One of the main concerns women expressed as they prepared to move out had been safety for themselves and their children. Five women had re-established and remained in contact with their abusers, either in accordance with court orders or informally, feeling that it was important for their children to remain in contact with their fathers. Gemma was in contact in order to see her two older children, who were now in their father's custody. Contact arrangements (discussed in Chapter 7) could run smoothly or provide occasion for further abuse, but meant that women knew where their abuser was and when contact might take place.

For the other women, no contact was involved, as they believed that their former partners did not know where they were. This had resulted in a continuing but more diffused fear in the background of their lives – a constant theme within many of the interviews and one that could, on rare occasions, temporarily take over their lives. Charmian, like others in the group, had changed the family name and was sure her abuser did not know where she was. But when the police telephoned her to say his current girlfriend had reported him missing, she was terrified:

> Because I just don't know what he's capable of…but I did have the fear of him being [here]. I even rang Jenny [FSW] and I says to her, 'Do you think I've owt to worry about?' So she says, 'No, I wouldn't have thought so.' But it didn't help. I were going like this all't time, looking behind me. You know, I was scared to go out. But after a week, I thought, whatever happens, happens.

Even when they had moved long distances to escape, women spoke of 'always looking over my shoulder' and of their fear of visiting busy city centres or any locality where the abuser might possibly visit, or where work might take them. This fear extended to the family of the abuser who, they felt, might mention seeing them or take action themselves. Leanne was emphatic:

> No, no, I wouldn't go back there for love nor money. My partner, she's now in prison…for a long time. But…um…there's the family and stuff like that. So, no, I wouldn't go back.

These self-imposed limitations did not dominate their lives, but could cause problems if they needed to attend interviews or court proceedings, or obtain documents – difficulties that were not always understood or handled with sensitivity by agencies.

For many of the women, whether they were in contact or not, this apprehension extended into the home. The safety plan they had prepared, in consultation with their support worker, gave some reassurance on the actions they could take if an incident occurred; nevertheless, there was still a generalised and uncertain fear that they were unable to explain, but that definitely existed in their minds. Maddy kept her doors and windows locked at all times; Sally had equipped all her family with mobile phones preprogrammed to the local police number. Sylvia, who had regular contact, still saw herself as needing to protect[12] her son at night:

> I mean I've got my bedroom. Not that I often sleep in it, I often sleep still down here, but that's a…I still think that's that slight insecurity thing going on, you know, 'cos I keep thinking, 'I've got a perfectly good bed upstairs now and I ought to be in it.' When we initially moved here it was that fear of retribution and the children being upstairs, that I wanted to be that…sounds ridiculous. And I don't think of it like that now, but it obviously is still that, 'cos when I go upstairs I feel

MANAGING A NEW LIFE / 101

quite uneasy that Daniel's room is before mine. And I know that is
absolutely ridiculous because I have no problems whatsoever now,
but it still has that kind of little resonating feeling inside me that I'm not
quite comfortable...that I'm not there, on guard as it were, like that
sleeping dog syndrome.

Sanctuary schemes[13] had not been introduced at the time these women left
the refuge, and although internal security systems, with panic alarms, can
be made available, only one of the women had such a system. There was
a general feeling, perhaps based on past experience, that nothing would
stop an abuser breaking in, if it came to it. And although these fears had
clearly originated from their experiences of abuse, they now seemed to be
extended to anyone who might violate their feeling of safety. Where these
fears were present, they did not seem to have diminished over time and
they remained a major concern for them at the time of our last meetings,
years after leaving the abusive relationship.

Concerns about safety, financial insecurity and the lack of opportunity
to improve their lives had been real concerns for all of these women as they
moved into their new communities. Over the period I knew them, some
had made substantial changes to their lives and had major achievements
to celebrate. Others still had some way to go. What had changed over the
years was their growing ability to deal with problems and people, even
when circumstances were against them, and a willingness to try. This was
not a smooth progression, and often their ability to cope with situations
was dependent on their physical and emotional health and the extent to
which this continued to be influenced by their past experiences.

Summary

- Managing on a low income required skill and determination.
  Keeping themselves and their children fed and clothed, but also
  being able to pay their household bills was a delicate balance,
  easily upset by sudden and unexpected increases or the need to
  replace or repair household equipment.

- The women's inability to provide for their children the small treats,
  clothing and equipment that would put them on equal terms with
  their peers was a source of frustration and distress.

- Where women were struggling to repay debts, either incurred
  during the relationship or subsequently, this was an added strain

on resources. Debt counsellors and support workers had provided advice and assistance in dealing with the situation, but women also suggested that specific life skills training in planning and managing their money before leaving the refuge would have been helpful.

- Although women saw employment as a route out of poverty, there were complex factors influencing their ability to seek and retain work. Among these were the intricacies of the benefits system and the lack of affordable and accessible childcare that was of good quality.

- Entering training or further education offered another option, but this was similarly constrained by cost and childcare considerations. Where loans were available, these would result in debts to be repaid at a later date.

- Voluntary work provided social contact and work experience, as well as a possible pathway into paid employment. It also helped women to overcome the self-doubt and lack of confidence that resulted from the abuse.

- The economic and social barriers that held women back from seeking employment caused frustration at their inability to improve their situation. This might result in their becoming 'stuck' and unable to move forward. Proposed government measures need to address these barriers if they are to be successful.

- Where women were studying or in work, they had gained confidence as a result of their achievements. Gaining qualifications was a sign of their worth and place in society, but they emphasised that this had not been an easy option.

- Providing short trips and holidays for themselves and their children was a struggle for those on a low income, and women felt guilty that they were depriving their children of the opportunities that others enjoyed. Camping and caravanning had provided inexpensive breaks; some had been able to access free holidays and others had been assisted by their extended families. These breaks had been of value to the whole family.

- Poverty also restricts access to other forms of social interaction and women's ability to take time out for themselves.

- Safety continued to be a concern for the women. Even when they had changed their names and moved long distances, they were wary of crowded locations or any locality where their abuser might have contacts. This fear extended into their homes and to anyone who might appear to violate their sense of safety. These fears were still in the background of their lives years after leaving the relationship.

Notes

1. There were varied reasons for this: some women had moved away from their place of work; for others, informal childcare arrangements were no longer possible. More importantly, even if staying in work were possible, the cost of staying in the refuge rose to a higher level than they could afford.

2. The struggle to survive on a low income has been a consistent theme in research into the lives of women who leave abusive relationships (Binney et al. 1981; Hoff 1990; Humphreys and Thiara 2002; Pahl 1985; Women's Budget Group 2008).

3. A study by the Women's Budget Group (2008) found that the inability to provide basic needs and small luxuries for their children was a source of deep anguish to women living in poverty.

4. A point also made by Charles (1994).

5. Government Equalities Unit 2008.

6. This desire has been reflected in other research findings (Abrahams 2004; Pahl 1985).

7. Walby and Olsen (2002) point out that women are over-represented in lower-paid jobs such as cleaning, shop work, childcare and routine clerical work, and that many work part time to meet the needs of their families. They further comment that this situation is exacerbated by the continuing inequality between the pay of men and women. This point has also been noted by the Government Equalities Unit (2008).

8. Similar findings come from Walby and Olsen (2002) and the Women's Budget Group (2008). As Maslow (1987) points out, social and economic barriers are a key element in preventing personal growth and development.

9. A major study, in 2008, on the costs of child poverty to society and the individual, was funded by the Joseph Rowntree Foundation. Within this study, Waldfogel and Garnham concluded that the lack of appropriate and accessible childcare, together with the complexities of the welfare payment system, formed significant

barriers to parents seeking work and lifting themselves and their children out of poverty.

10. In a further section of the study, Hirsch concluded that parental poverty severely limited children's access to activities enjoyed by their peers and that this may disadvantage children in many aspects of their later lives.

11. Earlier research (Abrahams 2007; Kirkwood 1993; McGee 2000b) has suggested that, once women were released from the abusive relationship, some of them showed a tendency to 'go wild'. Several years down the line, there was no evidence of this, although comments from some women indicated that something of this nature might have occurred earlier.

12. Similar patterns of night-time vigilance after leaving the relationship were noted by Lowe *et al.* (2007).

13. Sanctuary schemes are designed to provide additional security measures at doors and windows and, where possible, a 'safe room' within the house, with reinforced doors and bolts. They are designed to enable women who experience domestic violence and their children to remain safely in their own homes, if they so wish.

Chapter 6

Health and Well-being

The majority of the women who talked to me had suffered physical and sexual abuse, often carried to extremes, over many years. As our acquaintance deepened, I learnt more about the visible marks of violence that they still carried and I was also told of more intimate injuries that they had suffered. But it was the invisible scars, the effects of years of emotional abuse, that had, in their eyes, done the most damage. Because of the long-term nature of this project, women were meeting me for the second or third time. They had moved on in their own lives and were now ready to look back and talk to me about aspects of the abuse that at first had been too difficult to discuss or even think about. In successive interviews, I learnt more about the mental effects of their experiences and the ways in which this continued to have an impact on their lives.

Women talked of the coping behaviours they had adopted during the relationship to mask the physical and mental pain of abuse and help them endure the stress of their lives. These included a range of self-harming behaviours from smoking or the heavy use of alcohol, through self-medication with legal and illegal drugs, to causing themselves physical injury and suicidal behaviours. For a few of them, these strategies continued to be used, to an extent, after they had left the relationship. They also talked of the depression and sadness that could still shadow their lives, years after the abuse had ended.[1] For some of them, appropriate counselling had enabled them to start to place their experiences in context; for others, this had not felt appropriate or had not proved to be helpful. It had taken a long time for women to feel able to bring these previously hidden aspects of their lives into the light, but it was clear that these were matters they now felt able to talk about and that they wanted to give me a deeper picture of their lives, which could be used, as Sylvia said, so that 'others can understand where we're coming from, to help other women like me'.

Physical health

At the time that we first met, most of the women had left the abusive relationship comparatively recently and were still trying to come to terms with what had happened to them. Violence and abuse had resulted in poor physical health for many, both directly, in terms of physical violence directed against them, and indirectly, as a result of the diminished sense of self-worth resulting from emotional abuse, which had made it difficult for them to accept the need to care appropriately for themselves in terms of food, sleep and relaxation.

For years, many had put themselves at the 'bottom of the heap', working to meet the needs of their abuser and to care for the physical and emotional health of their children, with little to spare for themselves. Now they felt safe, both physically and mentally, and a growing sense of self-worth meant they valued and took care of themselves. In general, their sleep patterns improved, they ate regularly and sensibly, and were able to take exercise and relax. They also saw the importance of maintaining their physical health if they were to manage their new lives successfully, although some external factors could make this more difficult – as discussed in Chapter 5, it was hard to provide a healthy diet on a low income, and poverty also affected their ability to keep their houses warm during the winter months.[2] This latter problem was exacerbated where homes were still being brought up to standard, since there could be problems with damp or draughts; several women commented on recurring low-grade infections and minor illnesses – chest infections and the like – among their children, which they felt had resulted from these conditions.

Eight of the twelve women described themselves in their final interviews as physically fit and healthy. In Leanne's words, 'I'm fine. Brilliant. I've never felt better.' Three of them had joined their local gyms as one aspect of caring for themselves, and this had not only improved their physical condition and provided social interaction, but had had a positive effect on their mental outlook. 'It's fantastic,' Lindy said. 'Them endorphins work wonderfully!' For others, looking after their active children was exercise enough. And although Maddy and Sally both had chronic health problems unrelated to the abuse, they considered that, otherwise, their physical health was satisfactory and far better than when they were in the abusive relationship.

Gemma, as discussed later, was wrestling with physical reactions to a detoxification programme, and it was not possible to draw any conclusions as to her general health. Molly was the only woman whose health had deteriorated since she left the refuge, when, apart from asthma attacks, she considered her health had been good. With the help of her support worker, she had overcome her difficulties with other agencies, regained her confidence and started to study for qualifications. Some five years after leaving, however, she had collapsed while out shopping and subsequently had been diagnosed with major heart problems and associated conditions. Now permanently on oxygen and with a high level of medication, her activities were severely restricted, leading to anger and frustration at being so helpless, which she took out on those around her:

> Can't do no lifting… I can't even sort of…I have to sit down to cook a meal, which is ridiculous. Never done that…sit down to wash the pots? You know, it's like all my independence has been taken away.

Her worsening condition had meant that her last remaining child had had to go into care, and this final loss, added to all the others she had experienced, had deeply affected her. From feeling that her struggles had paid off and that she was creating new opportunities for herself, she was now becoming despondent and aware of her limited life expectancy:

> It's totally knocked me. I'm losing all my will to do anything. Sometimes I just want to give up and just say, 'Right, I've had enough. That's it, I just want to go. I don't want to be here.' I'm so scared at night to go to sleep because I'm scared I ain't going to wake up.

Torn between these conflicting emotions, Molly had twice exceeded her prescribed level of medication in the hope of resolving her dilemma, but also said that, at times, she was so exhausted that she could not remember what she had, or had not, taken. She was now pinning her remaining hopes on being able to move to the specially adapted housing she had been promised and on the possibility of support from her local mental health team. Although a previous assessment had not felt this was appropriate, her situation had again deteriorated and she believed she needed help at this stage of her life.

Coping behaviours and strategies

While they were in the abusive relationships, the women had experienced intense emotional pain and anguish. Feelings of despair, worthlessness and fear, of being powerless and alone, and of anger they dared not express could, at times, become overwhelming. As a way of relieving their emotional distress, numbing the pain they felt, and escaping, either permanently or temporarily, from the abusive situation, many of them resorted to actions and behaviours that had the potential to hurt or damage them in some way.[3] These included those generally regarded as self-harming, such as cutting or damaging their bodies, self-medication with legal and illegal drugs, and suicide attempts, but also other behaviours such as deliberate risk-taking and those that can be regarded as 'self-harm', but are, perhaps, seen in some circles as more socially or culturally acceptable,[4] such as smoking, heavy drinking or overworking.

As with their physical health, once women were out of the abusive situation, growing feelings of self-worth generally led to changes in self-harming activities, and as they learnt to value themselves, self-harm turned to self-care. Inflicting direct physical damage to their bodies was one of the coping behaviours that seemed to have lessened in intensity and then virtually stopped within a short space of time, once women felt physically and mentally safe in the refuge and were receiving understanding and support. Those who talked to me about this sort of action felt that they were unlikely to resort to it again, but knew that they could never totally rule it out. Briony, for example, had not self-harmed for five years, but could not say that it had permanently stopped; merely that it would only happen 'if things really got on top of me'.[5]

Many of the women had, at some point during the abuse, been prescribed tranquillisers or antidepressants by their doctors, and some also had painkillers for injuries they had sustained. For a few of them, using high levels of this sort of medication, either from prescriptions or from over-the-counter remedies, had provided a way of withdrawing from what was happening to them, but once out of the abusive situation, women said they felt less need for these drugs. Levels of use fluctuated, depending on the stresses they encountered, but most of them were actively trying to reduce any drug dependency and look for other ways to deal with their emotional needs.[6] A very small number of women had chosen to use illegal drugs and/or alcohol as their way of dulling the emotional pain they were experiencing, or as a way of temporary escape. Leanne described why she used drugs:

> Well, my ex had a really bad habit…and with all the beatings and that, it just got to the point where if I was out of my face, it didn't hurt so much. So I didn't have…a really bad habit, I just did it more as pain relief, if you want.

At the time of our last interviews, none of those who had reported using illegal drugs[7] in this way were still doing so, and alcohol was limited to the occasional social drink or none at all. This was especially so where their abuser had been a heavy drinker and women wanted to provide a better role model for their children.

Back from the brink

Thoughts of suicide had occurred to several of the women, sometimes occasionally, sometimes as a recurring theme, while they were in the abusive relationship; only two told me that they had actually tried to kill themselves during this time. One of these was Lindy who, although she had had clear ideas on a successful future for herself and her children from the time she entered the refuge, continued to be haunted by her suicidal thoughts and feelings during her first few months there:

> I'm just in limbo at the moment thinking...I think I've done the right thing, because I just...I just don't know nothing. I took an overdose a couple of weeks ago and ended up in hospital so...that's when I hit rock bottom. Come out, but I still am very up and down. I felt suicidal again, just...just want to give up. I'm trying. Lindy that's inside me is saying, 'Come on', but there's another Lindy sort of saying, 'Oh forget it, just don't do it no more.' It's hard.

Initially, she needed intensive support from her refuge worker, both in one-to-one sessions and by telephone when she felt herself to be again at risk. As she began to feel physically and mentally safe, this support, together with that from other residents, began to restore her confidence and belief in herself. She was able to reflect on what had happened and, six months later, described it as 'surreal' and something she would never contemplate again:

> No, they've gone. I'll never do that again. And I've said to the children... we used to have these lie down times on an evening, and if they wanted to ask anything, I promised I'd be totally honest. Anything they wanted to ask I'd tell them. And we lay there one night and Rose said, 'Mummy, you know when you' – I was poorly to them – 'when you were poorly' – I said, 'Yeah' – 'did you try to kill yourself?' I said, 'Yes, I did.' And it was 'Why?' – I couldn't answer her. I said, 'I was so sad, Rose.' She said, 'Well, why didn't you tell me you were sad?' I says, 'You couldn't have helped me.' And she went very quiet and she says, 'But you won't do it again, will you, Mum?' And I actually sort of sat back and looked at her and thought, 'No. I'll never let myself get that low again.'

Gemma, whose problems with relationships were discussed in Chapter 4, told me that she had attempted suicide on a number of occasions during her first abusive relationship. Later, it emerged that she had also used cutting herself and impulsively taking dangerous risks (for example, playing 'chicken' across major roads) as a way of dealing with her feelings of powerlessness and numbing the pain of sexual, physical and emotional abuse. Physical violence had resulted in permanent damage to her body for which she needed painkillers, and she had also been prescribed antidepressants. Both of these she had, at times, used to excess. And, although she described herself as appearing to be 'bubbly and outgoing', in reality, constant criticism and control over her life had destroyed her self-confidence and she felt she needed increasing amounts of alcohol to overcome her fear and anxiety in social settings.

After leaving this relationship these problems remained, but she began to bring them under control, with help and support from the local hospital. To do this was not easy for her, and if difficult situations, such as contact with her ex-husband or dealing with supporting agencies (other than with the refuge worker) arose, her use of self-medication increased. When her feelings of isolation and loneliness led to the start of a new relationship, which quickly became abusive, she returned to her earlier coping behaviours and the use of speed as an alternative to alcohol. Finally taking the decision to leave her home, and the relationship, offered a new start, far away from her abuser, but also meant the loss of her existing support systems. Shortly after leaving, she found she was again pregnant by her abuser, her drinking increased (although she did not resort to illegal drugs) and workers felt unable to support her within the refuge.[8] By this time, she had recognised that her physical and mental distress was such that she was unable to parent properly; her two older children had gone to their father and she agreed to place the two youngest, including her newborn baby, voluntarily in care. Gemma had always acknowledged that she had a drink problem, but this had now reached the stage where she was not able to stop and had been told that it could be dangerous to cut off completely. Her self-harming behaviours, including risk-taking, had returned, and her despair and anguish were extreme as she waited for a detox programme:

> I was prepared to do anything to get it done quicker...anything whatsoever...because I wanted to get better. I knew, with all the emotional stresses of my kids not being there, I could drink to the point of oblivion which would take...I could drink four litres of vodka

probably and end up dead. And I kept saying, 'I'm dying', you know, 'don't...can't you see, I don't want to die?' I just kept myself sober every day for contact. Then after that was done, pfff...I didn't want to know any more. Didn't want to know about the world, didn't want to know about life, it hurt too much.

The last time we met, Gemma was three weeks out of the detox programme she had wanted so much. She was now beginning to experience the pain of withdrawal, but also the benefits of life without alcohol:

I get that pang, especially when my heart hurts and I'm feeling...I just want to cry for the pain, and I bottled it inside for so long and then I bottled it in a bottle if you like. Um...and it was, but I'll tell you something, a bottle of vodka is no conversationalist...crap jokes as well! So I'm much better having real people as my companion than vodka.

Clearing the alcohol out of her system had enabled her to think more clearly about her other problems, including her use of medication, her risk-taking and her mental well-being. She had been referred to the local Mental Health Assessment Team, and a full assessment had resulted in the offer of Dialectical Behavioural Therapy (DBT),[9] which she hoped would have positive benefits for her relationships with others. She was beginning to see that there could be a new life ahead for her:

At the end of the day I can't change the situation about the kids, all I can do is change myself and get myself better, so that they've got no excuses. And that means being frank... It was me feeling safe again. Me believing in myself again, me loving myself, looking after myself. Just finding friends and things. It was so...being cared about by other people as well and not being abused, and me not allowing it. And doing AA, the fact that I am doing things...you know being sober opens so many doors, it does. People want to help you, they want you to stay dry, they want...you know, as long as you don't take the piss out of that, and you only ask when you really are struggling or whatever, then um...then they're not going to...you know. They're going to be there and that you can make some good friendships..

Staying sober and choosing self-care over self-harm will, as Gemma recognises, be a major change that can have the potential to turn her life around, but it will take courage and determination to sustain. At the same time, she faces massive practical challenges – court hearings concerning her children's future (where her mental health assessment may play a key role), finding a new home and gaining employment. All of these will test her strengths to the limit and she will need appropriate and long-term support if she is to succeed.

Women like Gemma, who experience domestic violence and abuse, but also have mental health problems and, perhaps, issues of self-harm and dependencies, have complex support needs. Their individual problems overlap, but the services they need tend to be compartmentalised, focusing on a single issue, without necessarily considering the context and wider implications.[10] From Gemma's perspective, as discussed in Chapter 3, this appeared to be what was happening to her: she was being seen by a number of agencies, each concerned with one aspect of her situation. This added to her sense of confusion and made it difficult for her to work with them, especially if their priorities conflicted. A coordinated approach, linking to additional informal support, would appear to offer the best chance of a successful outcome for these families.

Easing the pain in daily life

Other coping mechanisms that women used during the abusive relationship and that continued, to some extent, after leaving are less easily seen as self-harming. Seven mentioned their attitude and approach to food during the period of the abuse. Some had found comfort in eating; others had seen regulating their food intake as a means of exercising some element of control over their restricted lives. A further complication was the way in which their abuser had been able to exercise control over diet – explicitly, by restricting the cash available or specifying what could be eaten by the family, or implicitly, by criticism of their weight and general appearance.[11] Leaving offered women the opportunity to change the relationship between themselves and food. This was not an easy task. Initially, some women ate to excess because they were free to do so; others chose previously forbidden foods, or ate to comfort themselves in this new and frightening world; and others, again, were too distressed to eat at all. In successive visits, I witnessed both substantial gains and losses of weight, as women learnt to care for themselves and take back control over their own bodies. During this time, there were no indications from any of them that they felt in need of treatment for eating disorders – they were finding out for themselves how they wanted to be.

For those women who had been allowed to do so, work had provided social contact and a relief from the abusive situation. It had given Keira a way of separating her working self from the woman[12] who was being abused:

> I was living two very different lives. It was really strange how I'd split myself in two where I could completely switch off with what Doug was doing to me… Doug was doing that to me, but the Keira that walked out in the morning to go to a job with a suit on and covering her bruises with the make-up was a different person…and that's how I think I survived. And if I'm truthful, Hilary, I think my strength was my weakness at that point. Because I think I would have walked out a long time ago.

She took every opportunity to carry out additional work, business trips and conferences until a final incident drove her into leaving the abusive relationship. The refuge had given her a space to reflect on her priorities and resulted in a complete change in her lifestyle:

> And then because I couldn't [go to work] I sat back and reflected on it and realised, 'What was I doing anyway?' I was very work-orientated, now I'm not. And I think that's been for the better.

Smoking was probably the most common and widely adopted coping behaviour. All but two of the women had been regular smokers and saw tobacco as having been one of the essentials of their daily lives. Leaving the relationship was often the trigger for an increase in cigarette consumption; many remembered chain-smoking during the early days at the refuge, but felt strongly that this had not been a time to place additional stress on themselves by giving up. A week into her stay, Lindy told me, 'I've gone from like eight a day to about 30 at the moment. It's not the time to pack in, it's just my bit of sanity.'

Even after they had left the abusive relationship, smoking was seen as a way of coping with the stresses and strains caused by poverty, frustration and the problems of living independently. After a number of years, as things became more stable in their lives, consumption generally fell, but was still liable to fluctuate, as Jeannie explained:

> It goes up and down, it depends how I'm feeling really, do you know what I mean? It's really difficult. Like yesterday I only had like three cigarettes for the whole day. And then like sometimes I'll smoke six, seven, eight, nine, ten. It depends how I feel.

Ten a day was, in fact low compared to some of the other women, who said they had, at times, peaked at anything up to 40 a day. At the time we last met, six women had become very occasional smokers, either socially or to relax after a particularly stressful day. Lindy and Charmian had stopped altogether, linking this clearly to how they felt about themselves in their new lives. Charmian said, 'I just stopped. I thought I'm not doing this, this is me now, you know, this is who I am and I'm not doing it.' Briony had also stopped, although she ruefully admitted this was a second attempt and she felt it was too early to say if this would last.

Taking a stand

Women adopted these coping behaviours as a way of dealing with the internal stresses that the abuse caused them. They also adopted a number of external strategies to modify and avoid, as far as possible, situations that might be occasions for violence and abuse directed at them or their children. Much of this involved modifying their own behaviours: acting to please and satisfy the abuser, meeting their demands, defusing tensions and potential flashpoints. The driving aim was to avoid actions that might be seen by the abuser as confrontational or challenging. Once they had left the relationship, a key aspect of independent living was the need to rebuild their confidence and learn to self-advocate in a variety of situations. On occasions, however, this had to be taken further, and women had to confront and challenge behaviours and attitudes that they found unacceptable.

Initially, this was immensely difficult and frightening for them, given the violent responses that had resulted from such actions in the past. It was made even more difficult if the person concerned was male, whatever the gender of their abuser had been. Women described the almost paralysing fear that gripped them and the physical reactions that characterise panic attacks – dry mouth, shaking hands and difficulty in breathing.[13] Gradually, as their own sense of self-worth increased, the difficulties inherent in tackling these problems became less; women found that being assertive did not necessarily result in violence, and taking action rather than being a passive recipient positively enhanced their feelings of self-esteem. It was still, however, not an easy task to take this action. Charmian, who had learnt helpful breathing techniques at an assertiveness group, said, 'I am a bit more stronger in myself, you know, I can stick up for myself when I need to. But it doesn't stop me from shaking and getting the jitters.' These panic attacks did, also, sometimes occur in other circumstances that evoked unsettling memories – for example, suddenly seeing someone who, on first sight, appeared to be their abuser – but these episodes became fewer over the years.

Good days, bad days

The emotional well-being of all of the women was probably at one of its lowest points when I first met them in the refuge. First and foremost, they were wrestling with the impact of uprooting themselves and their children and of leaving the relationship. As I have suggested earlier, this was similar to the initial impact of bereavement, with feelings of shock, numbness, unreality, disbelief and a profound sense of loss. At this point, women spoke of being unable to think and of 'being a complete wreck'. And underlying these immediate feelings was the damage caused by abuse to their feelings of personal worth and autonomy. Feelings of depression and hopelessness, springing from their low self-esteem and lack of confidence, were evident, with more than half of them having already been prescribed antidepressants during the period of the abuse. Feeling safe, accepted and supported within a community where everyone understood the mental and physical effects of domestic violence and abuse enabled them to begin the process of recovery.

Moving out into the community tested their developing strengths, and previous chapters have shown the value of continued support as women took on the practical and emotional challenges of a new life. But, as Briony commented, this support could only go so far; further progress was up to the woman herself and would take place over a much longer period:

> Yeah, you go in and you're a wreck. And then, when you've been there for a time, you come to terms with what's happened. And you build up your new life, you sort of get it sorted in your own way.

It was once this period of support was over and life began to settle into more of a pattern, that women seemed to become aware that they were not getting over things as easily as they had thought they would. They had feared being alone, they had feared the responsibility of taking decisions and they had feared being found. What they had not expected was the way in which memories of the abuse continued to cast shadows of anxiety and depression over them. Feelings of anger and hate, which had been bottled up for years, to avoid making matters worse, began to appear,[14] and women found this, in itself, frightening. Briony was the only woman whose anger had, occasionally, exploded while in the relationship – 'Holding things in, and then one day you can't cram anything else in and it just...' – but she, too, had been afraid of her own fury. And these emotions were often compounded by the constant anxiety of struggling on a low income.

The intensity of these feelings did begin to change over time. Some two years after she had left the relationship, Jeannie was struggling to cope with feelings of distress that sometimes overwhelmed her and to focus on the future for herself and her children:

> Life has to go on. It has to go on. Whether you feel great, or you feel like…you know. It has to go on. And don't get me wrong, sometimes I'll sit here and I'm just crying for the whole day, sometimes the whole weekend. I'll just like, 'Oh my God.' But then I just get myself back up again and think, 'No, you've just got to be strong for the kids,' you know.

At the time of our last discussions, two years later, she was beginning to feel better about herself, but still experienced difficulties from time to time:

> I sort of get down a little bit, I still get depressed, but, you know, I'm not bitter. Before I was bitter, I felt…oh that's it, I was quite bitter… angry and bitter, and I'm not any more.

The majority of the women expressed similar shifts in their feelings, with ten of them talking of having 'good days and bad days'. For some, these feelings were hardly ever in evidence. 'Oh, I still have bad days,' said Leanne, 'but not…whereas I used to wake up every morning and it's the first thing I thought about. And now I don't. I can go days without thinking and it's brilliant.' Others, like Keira, found that their emotions were of immense sadness and regret:

> Now at times, if I can sit here… But I could get quite sad about it all, if I'm really honest. Things that I've gone through, things the children have gone through…that I let it go on for so long…

She and two other women commented that often these emotional responses were triggered by advertisements on television that brought back memories and feelings – not necessarily of the abuse, but of the good times within the relationship or of all they had lost.

Even when there were far more good days than bad days, there were times when these feelings could strike out of the blue, with devastating effects. Four years after leaving, Sally found that she could be totally incapacitated by her reactions:

> Some days I have real bad days. 'Cos I'm not on any medication 'cos I find they make me worse. So I'm just trying to try it myself. Some days I have just to stay in bed. And other days I can be out in the garden loving it.

It was not easy for women to admit, even to themselves, that the past was still affecting them. Sylvia, two years after leaving, told me that she just did not want to talk about her feelings to other people. 'I want just to move forward, because it's pointless, all this hate and anguish…you can't live like that, it just destroys you, doesn't it?' Briony expressed similar thoughts: 'Why live…there's no point living in the past, you've got to get on with it now. That's just what we're doing.'

Both of these women, however, and three others, had come to realise that they needed to unravel and understand the past, in order to move forward, and that to do so required support from elsewhere.

Someone to listen

Counselling[15] had been available for most women during the time they had been in the refuge, but not all of them had chosen, or been able, to go down this path, and, for others, it had not proved to be the right choice at that time. For Keira and Maddy, the support of other women, the opportunity to talk freely and the space to reflect had been sufficiently therapeutic in themselves, as Keira explained:

> There was lots of issues in my life that I'd not really dealt with… And I felt that there was one or two people in [the refuge] that I could confide in. And things that I never thought I'd ever talk about again…I actually did talk about and I found that very therapeutic. But once I'd gone past that, I was ready to move on.

Jeannie had very much wanted counselling while in the refuge, to explore her past experiences in depth, but, because of the need to move to different refuges, she had not been able to access these services. Currently in temporary accommodation, she saw little point in trying again at this point in her life. Counselling had not been available within their refuges either for Molly or Gemma, but both, as discussed earlier, were now looking for assistance with a different set of problems.

Leanne and Charmian had both worked with a counsellor during the latter part of their stay in the refuge, but had decided, fairly rapidly, that the counsellor's focus on their past life and experiences had not been the best route for them at that time. Looking back on her sessions, Leanne felt it had stressed her out: 'Talking about it…it just brings it all back. I'd rather just put it in the past and forget about it.' She had not sought further counselling but, as her comments earlier in this chapter show, she was gradually finding her own way of moving on. Charmian had reacted in a similar way to one-to-one counselling, but had joined an assertiveness group on leaving the refuge. Initially, this had proved very helpful, but had ultimately moved too fast into areas she had not wanted to explore. She was, however, using the knowledge she had gained to move forward at her own pace.

Of the five women who had engaged with counselling after leaving the refuge, only Liz had also done so while a resident. She and Sylvia had been recommended to counsellors linked to their refuges, while Sally and Briony had been referred to counsellors attached to their GP's practice. For Sally, counselling had not met her needs, since the counsellor had focused on her present and future, and on learning ways to manage her feelings and move forward, whereas she felt strongly that she needed to explore and understand the past, before she could do this:

> I've had counselling and that didn't really help. She kept asking me about my future, not my past. And it was my past I wanted to talk about, not my future. Because I don't know what's going to happen in my future. I know what's happened in my past, but I don't know what's going to happen in the future. I wanted to talk about my past, I wanted to get it out in the open. So it's not all blocked up, blocked up in my mind all of the time. Because it seems to be locked away and then some days it'll just come and that's when I have real bad days. But she just didn't seem to…I felt she didn't really want to know. Soon as I was in there I was out again really. I had six weeks and that's all she wanted to give me. That's not long enough.

She was reluctant, despite the emotional pain she was experiencing, to seek further help. The other three (Briony, Sylvia and Liz) had been able, with support from their counsellors, to explore and understand their past experiences. Talking to their counsellor in this way had not been easy, as Sylvia had found: 'Well, I learned for ten years not to give anything away, and that is a hard habit to break. Even though now I don't need to hide anything.' All of them felt, however, that ultimately, it had been a life-changing experience. Liz had appreciated her earlier counselling sessions, but had gained even more from this later experience:

> I've got to admit if anything out of life…them sessions with her were the best ever what has put my mind straight… It makes you think

about yourself, makes you question things, and it makes you look at things differently. And I come out a more confident, stronger-willed person than I actually were before.

Lindy had taken a different path to any of the others: she had enrolled on a local counselling course. In learning the skills of counselling and reflecting on her experience, both alone and in groupwork, she had reached a greater understanding of her own situation. As with all of the women in this study, however, she was well aware that there was no quick fix. The past could still have an impact on their present lives, and each of them was drawing on their own strengths to find their individual ways to cope with this.

The accounts of the women who accessed counselling after leaving the refuge confirm my earlier findings (Abrahams 2007) that this had a different focus from the counselling work carried out within the refuge. Often building on earlier thoughts and reflections, women brought a different perspective to counselling once they had started to live independently. New situations arose, feelings previously suppressed began to surface and women themselves had changed, wanting to look at different aspects of their experiences and bringing different understandings and a greater ability to reflect on themselves and their lives.

Whether they had chosen to work with a counsellor or not, and whatever their experiences of this had been, all of the women felt strongly that this form of support should be widely available, both in refuges and once they had moved back into the community,[16] but that taking this path had to be a matter for personal choice. Each of these women had individual needs that changed at different times in their lives, and they wanted to be able to access the services they felt were right for them at any particular time. They knew what they needed in terms of personal support, and when they were ready to move from one type of support to another, when supportive networks were the best option and when they felt a need for individual counselling or groupwork. Equally, they knew when these were not appropriate.

Counselling has been shown to be helpful to many individuals in a variety of situations,[17] but, as these women's accounts indicate, no one therapeutic approach works best for everyone: some of those in this project felt a deep need to explore and understand the past; others may have preferred support in moving forward. And, for some women, like Keira and Maddy, peer support may be all they need. With so many differing theoretical approaches to talking therapies available, it is important that women can access the right model and style for them and also that they can establish a good working relationship with the counsellor. For individuals who have experienced domestic violence and abuse, it is equally important that the counsellor fully understands the effect and impact this is likely to have had and is able to provide a safe therapeutic space in which they can explore their issues.[18]

Barriers to seeking help

The physical and, in particular, the emotional effects that abuse had had on the women came through with great clarity in their stories. They drew on a variety of sources for support, but were generally wary of seeking help from recognised medical professionals. Some of this reluctance clearly stemmed from past experience: a few women had received support and understanding, but others had felt that GPs did not want to know about the abuse and simply prescribed medication, looking only at the presenting problem rather than asking about the context in which this occurred.[19]

More significant were their fears around mental health interventions. Their abusers had repeatedly told them they were 'crazy', 'mad', or 'losing their marbles'. For them to be diagnosed with mental health problems and become involved with formal mental health procedures offered the prospect of reinforcing these messages, particularly since they were now coming from those seen as authority figures. Already nervous of revealing their experiences of abuse to others, women feared being further labelled and subsequently stigmatised in the eyes of those around them, concerned that this might lead to them and their mental health being regarded as 'the problem', rather than seeing their mental distress as a direct consequence of abuse. A further and very real fear, as Gemma's comments show, was that diagnosis and treatment, including medication, might lead to concerns about their ability to parent and could be used against them in civil or criminal proceedings[20] involving access to, or custody of, their children.

Fears of this nature, as with those concerning other statutory agencies and organisations, could deter women from contacting potential sources of help. Wherever possible, they preferred to draw on their own growing strength and inner resources and on less formal social support from those around them – family, friends, the local community and support groups – to rebuild their lives and those of their children.

Summary

- At the time they left the relationship, many women were in poor physical health. For the majority, their health gradually improved as they regained respect for themselves and recognised the need to care for themselves.

- Many of the women had resorted to self-harming behaviours during the period of the abuse, including self-mutilation, the use of legal and illegal drugs, attempted suicide and deliberate risk-taking. These behaviours were used to relieve the intense emotional anguish they felt. It also gave them some control in a situation where they felt powerless. As self-care replaced self-harm, these behaviours reduced or stopped.

- Other behaviours that can be seen as self-harm, but may appear more socially and culturally acceptable, included overworking, heavy drinking and smoking. The latter was something that continued for some time after being rehoused and was regarded as essential in coping with the stresses they encountered in their lives. In general, the level of use gradually reduced.

- While in the abusive relationship, women had modified their behaviours to avoid confrontation and the possibility of further violence. After leaving, learning to confront unacceptable behaviour from others was difficult and could lead to panic attacks. As women learnt that being assertive did not normally result in violence, their self-esteem grew and these attacks lessened.

- Where women have complex needs resulting from the abuse (such as dependencies and mental health problems), it can be difficult for them to access appropriate services. Many agencies are 'single focus' and fail to take into account the overall context in which the presenting problem is situated.

- Most of the women suffered from recurring bouts of intense depression and sadness. Although these lessened over the years, they could still strike without warning and be overwhelming.

- Counselling had been helpful for a number of women, but all of them felt that this should be readily available for those who wanted it. The focus needed to be different for each woman and for the same woman at different times of her life, and counselling needed to be flexible enough to deal with this. It was also essential that the counsellor fully understood the effects of domestic violence and abuse, and was able to maintain a safe environment for them.

- Women were extremely wary of seeking assistance from medical professionals, fearing, in particular, that any involvement with mental health services might reflect badly on them when it came to civil or criminal court proceedings.

Notes

1. Higher levels of depression and self-harming actions and behaviours, including suicide, have been noted among women subject to domestic violence and abuse (Humphreys and Thiara 2003; Stark and Flitcraft 1996; Stevens and McDonald 2000).

2. Similar points were made in the report of the Women's Budget Group (2008).

3. Self-harming actions and behaviours are seen cross-culturally and are normally adopted as a consequence of the abuse rather than indicating any prior dependency (Barron 2004; Batsleer et al. 2002; Heath 2003; Sanderson 2008; Siddiqui 2003).

4. Arnold and Magill 2000; Turp 2003.

5. Arnold and Magill 2000. Sanderson (2008) points out the difficulty inherent in giving up a behaviour that has proved helpful in the past.

6. Humphreys and Thiara (2003) comment that diagnosis and medication is a central part of the medical model of treatment. They found that, although a few women welcomed the relief provided by antidepressants, many were not impressed with this as a response to their emotional distress and that medication needed to be seen as a part of a more holistic approach.

7. Using or supplying drugs was not tolerated in any of the refuges. Policy on alcohol varied, but excessive use was never acceptable.

8. As discussed in Chapter 2 (Note 10), few refuges have suitable facilities for women with complex needs, nor the specially trained staff required to offer the necessary degree of support (Barron 2004).

9. Dialectical Behavioural Therapy is one of a range of a third generation of Cognitive Behavioural Therapies (CBT) and was developed originally by Linehan and colleagues to treat complex mental disorders, such as Borderline Personality Disorder (BPD) and linked disorders, including substance dependencies, depression and suicidal tendencies. It utilises individual and group work, behavioural therapy and mindfulness techniques, and emphasises behavioural change, self-acceptance and emotional regulation (Cooper 2008; Dimeff and Linehan 2001). BPD is a diagnosis 'usually applied to women and associated with histories of child sexual abuse, self-harm and suicide' (Itzin 2006, p. 20).

10. Barron (2004), in a major survey of these services, found that they tended to focus on the presenting problem without considering the wider implications of the situation. Although a growing number of services were taking proactive approaches to complex problems and there were some excellent areas of good practice, service provision in general appeared to be patchy and inadequate. Recognition of the links between domestic abuse and mental health by the Department of Health/National Institute for Mental Health in England and the programme of work now being carried out to equip services to identify and respond to these needs (Itzin 2006) will, it is hoped, bring further impetus to the provision of these services.

11. See also Herman (2001) and Sanderson (2008).

12. Sanderson (2008) comments that this compartmentalisation is typical of high-achieving survivors.

13. Rothschild (2000) refers to the way in which the memory of past traumatic events is held both in the body and brain, creating instinctive physical reactions to future events that appear to be similar in nature.

14. Walker 1993; Dutton 1992. Acknowledging these feelings is seen as an important part of recovery (Herman 2001; Sanderson 2008).

15. As used here, 'counselling' describes a formal and agreed relationship between two people to meet at set times, within clear boundaries and with a mutual understanding of confidentiality, to work on specific aims connected with self-understanding and personal growth (Bond 2000; British Association for Counselling and Psychotherapy 2002). Counsellors are usually trained and belong to a professional body with a code of ethics to which they are expected to adhere.

16. Women's demands for accessible counselling are confirmed by a wide range of research – Abrahams 2007; Batsleer et al. 2002; Coleman and Guildford 2001; Humphreys and Thiara 2003; Lodge, Goodwin and Pearson 2001.

17. Cooper 2008.

18. A point emphasised by practitioners and researchers alike (Arnold and Magill 2000; Sanderson 2008).

19. See also Note 6. This may gradually change with the initiatives being taken across the NHS to encourage appropriate questioning and supportive action (Barron 2004; Feder et al. 2009; Williamson 1999).

20. A number of practitioners and researchers have recorded the way in which a diagnosis of mental health problems can be seen as pejorative and lead to victim blaming, with the possibility of negative effects in court proceedings (Barron 2004; Herman 2001; Humphreys and Joseph 2004; Rothschild 2000; Stark and Flitcraft 1996).

Chapter 7

And What About the Children?

The eight-year span of this study focused on the support needs and outcomes for women who had experienced domestic violence and abuse. It is not possible, however, to gain a full picture of their lives without considering the consequences of abuse for their children, since all were mothers, and their concerns and hopes for their children were a central focus of their lives. Whether children were currently with them, were independent adults or were being cared for by others, it was often their welfare that women were most concerned with and their needs that gave them the motivation to keep going and build a better future. They were acutely aware of the emotional turmoil that their children had gone through: first from witnessing or suffering abuse, then by leaving their homes, schools and friends, adjusting to life in the refuge, and, finally, settling into yet another new environment. They felt a sense of guilt at what had happened and the adverse effects this might have had, but also a pride in their sons and daughters and a fierce determination to do everything possible to give them a fresh start. Ending the relationship and the consequent removal of the fear of violence in their lives was a key element in this.

Many of the children had clearly been affected by the abuse, displaying behavioural and emotional difficulties for which women wanted to access appropriate services to help them recover. The women were also aware of the possible effects of abuse on their own relationship with their children, and the work that was needed to enable the family to develop and move forward together. For some families, contact arrangements had been a vehicle for continued abuse, delaying this process, although others had been able to negotiate mutually acceptable arrangements, which developed as children grew older. And, as time went on, new patterns evolved both within the family and with the wider community.

On leaving

When they left the abusive relationship and came to a refuge, the twelve women in this study had a total of 23 children with them: three women had brought one child each, seven had two children with them, and two were accompanied by three children. Of the children and young people, eight were aged five or under (including two under twelve months), ten were between the ages of six and ten, three were under 15, and there were two girls of 16 and 19.

Other children not physically present in the refuge were also closely involved with their mothers and affected by the change: both Lindy and Charmian had adolescent daughters from a previous relationship, who were living with their fathers. The girls remained in contact by phoning and texting and resumed visiting after the family was rehoused. Keira and Maddy had older, adult children who had long since left home and were living independent lives. Maddy's son had helped her to access the refuge and remained in contact, as did Keira's son and daughter, who had been well aware of the violence directed at their mother throughout her marriage. And there were other children who were never physically present, but nevertheless had a place in the family story: Sally had a son in kinship care, and Molly a son and daughter, together with three older children who had been adopted. These children remained very real to their mothers and were spoken of with sadness and regret as being permanently lost to them.

What domestic violence meant for the children

Research over the years has shown that children are aware of, and affected by, violence within their homes from a very early age,[1] even when mothers feel that they have concealed what is happening. They are distressed and bewildered, not only by the physical and sexual abuse directed at their mother, but also the inherent emotional violence and the tension and anxiety that permeates the atmosphere in the home. Two of the women in this study had thought that their children had not been aware of what was happening and were later devastated to discover the effect it had had on them. The remainder knew that their children had been aware of the physical and other abuse directed against them by a current or previous partner, sometimes being present while the abuse took place, at other times fully aware of what was going on downstairs or in the next room.[2]

Keira described how over 30 years of violence had been known to her four children:

> I mean, he's broken my ribs, he's knocked my teeth out, he's rubbed my face across the floor because his dinner…not that it wasn't cooked right, but there was not a sausage on it that he wanted. You know, I've gone through the whole shooting match with him, absolutely everything. My older children…my older children would see, on virtually a nightly basis, him put a chair up at the door, send them out and beat me while they were in one room and I was in another…so they've seen so much and heard so much. The beatings…those severe beatings, got less, his temper got less, but maybe the mental cruelty came in a little bit more then.

Children, even when very young, might also intervene (risking their own safety) to try to help their mothers, or fetch help, like Gemma's preschool daughter: '…because Anna has, actually…you know, she's stood in front of me and she has defended me to him before.'

A clear link has been established between domestic violence and the likelihood of children being abused, and three women specifically mentioned that there had been direct physical abuse of their children (sometimes to only one child in the family) by the person who was abusing them. Sexual abuse had occurred in one family, for which a conviction had been obtained, and had been suspected in another, without sufficient evidence to prosecute. Emotional abuse of children and young people was endemic; often they were subjected by the abuser to a strict control over what they could or could not do, and denied the freedom and activities natural to them. Sally explained:

> When I was with him, they weren't allowed out. They were allowed just in the back garden. Like Cathy…being her age, she wanted to be out with her friends. Her dad only lived up the road and she wanted to see him, but she wasn't allowed to see him.

Disobedience might be punished by destruction of their toys or property or by physical retribution directed either at them or their mothers. Like some of the other mothers, Sally had been strict with her children and feared to show them affection, in order to avoid any pretext for abuse from their partner. This had damaged their relationship with their children and could also be seen as continuing the abuse.

The consequences of abuse

Children and young people living with domestic violence and abuse inhabit an unsafe and unpredictable world, with feelings and experiences that can be hard to process at any age. In leaving, they also have to handle the loss of their existing world: family and friends, familiar schools and surroundings, toys and personal possessions. As Humphreys and Thiara (2002, p. 33) comment, these are 'children and young people whose lives have been disrupted emotionally, physically and materially by domestic violence'. Not surprisingly, the effects of this inner and outer turmoil became more visible after leaving the violence, when it felt safer for them to express their feelings, and mothers spoke of encountering a variety of behavioural and emotional problems among their children. These seemed to vary by age but not by gender; in general, the younger children (those under ten) appeared openly to demonstrate more behavioural and emotional problems than older children, adolescents and young adults. Some of the preschool children were described as 'clingy' and unwilling to let their mothers out of their sight for a considerable time after they had been rehoused, and two had developed speech impediments during the abuse, which were taking some time to disappear. A few had become quieter and withdrawn, while others (both boys and girls) became angry and aggressive towards their mothers and other people, and generally disruptive in their behaviour. Two of the youngest children seem to have been among the most seriously affected. Sally's young son had been four when she entered the refuge:

> I'm fighting to get him statemented at the moment because he's got global development disorder. Like he was a four year old and he's eight. Um...ADHD, anxiety...and there's another two that I can't remember. He needs to go into a special school because he's still doing reception work and he's going up to Year 4 in September and he's not going to be able to cope. What with all his class doing their age group, but he's doing four-year-old work.

Charmian, whose partner had 'left her for dead most nights', had left when her son was just two:

> I mean...he isn't as bad now than what he was when I first came here. 'Cos when I first came he was...I don't know how I got through it. He was a nightmare. I mean I were cracking up, because I didn't think I'd be able to get through it. He were getting ornaments and smashing them together and emptying the cutlery drawers all over the kitchen. He were just doing anything and everything to annoy me.

Five years later, things were beginning to show some improvement:

> So I'm more concentrating on bringing Andrew up and trying to get him right, 'cos he's having a lot of problems. He's still having speech therapy. He's still going to see a paediatrician for his attitude, and he's still wetting the bed now and again. He can be quite violent sometimes. But I just have to try and restrain him and say, 'No, that's not how you do it.' Try and calm him down a bit.

Being rehoused, the establishment of a predictable routine and a continuing sense of safety had been as important for the children and young people as it had been for their mothers, in helping them to begin to make sense of their lives again. As Liz explained, when we first met, 'Kids are getting used to not having violent surroundings and their personalities are coming through, so it's just building up, being able to relax and be who we really are.' A number, principally of the older children and young people, appeared to have come through their experiences relatively unscathed, but their mothers were aware that having been part of a violent household would have left its mark to some extent and expressed concern about how this might affect them at a later date.[3]

By the time of our last meetings, most of the mothers who had previously identified behavioural and emotional difficulties were happy with the changes that were taking place. For some, like Sally and Charmian, there was still a way to go, and other children still 'acted out' from time to time, but the majority were thriving in the new environment and their mothers were extremely proud of them. Sylvia was typical:

> It is that feeling that I've got them back centred and that, to me as a mum, is everything to me. You know, if I had nothing and I could look at them and think, 'They're not going to be me, they're going to be strong but still kind and truthful and good people, but with a bit more strength.'

Those who had been children and adolescents when they came to a refuge were now becoming teenagers and young adults, and a few, now in their mid-teens, had developed challenging behaviours. Their mothers were inclined to think that this was far more likely to be normal adolescent behaviour, rather than a delayed reaction to the domestic violence. 'We still have the normal mother/teenage tantrums,' Keira said, 'but that's life, we'd get that anyway, wouldn't we, whatever it was we were doing.'

Exploring close relationships outside the family is also a part of growing up and can be immensely difficult for young people, whether or not they have experienced domestic violence and abuse. It is not possible to say how their earlier experiences may ultimately affect their future relationships, but there were indications that these young people were thinking carefully about themselves and their relationships. Sylvia's daughter had ended a relationship when she realised it had the potential to become abusive:

> And one thing that I was so proud of her for – she came in one morning and said, 'I phoned him and kicked him out, kicked him to touch.' And I went, 'What?' She went, 'Yeah.' She goes, 'I thought about what you'd been saying' – 'cos I'd been dropping little hints, but I didn't want to upset her. And I'm thinking, 'Who am I to talk?' – you see, that's what I always revert back to – 'Who am I to talk?' – and I was so proud that she'd empowered herself, even though she liked him, to know that it wasn't going anywhere and that, you know, get out now and don't suffer years and years like I did, hoping there's going to be something that there's not going to be in realistic terms…and I was so proud of her. Although it made her unhappy, the pride was the empowerment she took from it – 'I'm not going to be like Mum, he's messing me about, he's history. There's more fish in the sea.' And I'm thinking, 'Yes, well done you.'

Other mothers felt that their adolescent daughters were being equally cautious about relationships, but they themselves were also monitoring the situation. Those with sons did not express concerns that they might become abusers; indeed, two of the boys had, on several occasions, expressed their determination not to become like their fathers.[4] 'I'm never going to treat a woman like you've been treated, Mum,' Patrick had told his mother. This was a very small group of young adults, but their thoughts about their future relationships are similar to those voiced in a larger study (Mullender *et al.* 2002).

Services

Women recognised that the effects of abuse on their children might feel very different from their own experiences, but could be equally as devastating in their impact and long-term consequences. They were aware that their sons and daughters might be in need of support to help the process of recovery, but many, like Lindy, felt that these needs might not easily be met:

It's hard on them. They just...they adapt, don't they, but...they're the forgotten people in all this, I think. There's support for the mums and the women, you know, but the children seem to be the forgotten people, they just have to keep going. It's sad.

Lindy's refuge did not, at that time, have a specialist children's worker, although one was appointed shortly after she left. All the other refuges had at least one worker dedicated to working with children, and a separate space, appropriately furnished, for their use. Mothers recognised that sessions with these workers were far more than just play, providing an opportunity for them to meet others with similar experiences, talk to workers if they wished, and generally relax in a supportive and safe environment. The role of the children's worker was particularly valued by mothers when they first came into the refuge, since, although they were concerned for their children, the effects of the abuse, the mental stress of leaving and immediate practical considerations could make it difficult for them to respond to their children's emotional needs.

The benefits to the children often became clear very quickly: 'It's done my Nigel a power of good since he's been going down there,' said Leanne, 'and even the staff have seen a big improvement.' This, in turn, as workers commented, helped women to relax, feel that they had done the right thing in leaving, and be more able to tackle their own problems. Facilities varied from refuge to refuge, with younger children generally well provided for in terms of creative play and activities. Those with older children would have liked more activities and facilities for them, such as quiet rooms for homework and more computer access, although they appreciated that the lack of space and resources made this difficult. (New-build and refurbished refuges are able to take these needs into account, but limited resources can restrict their provisions elsewhere.)

Lindy's comments that children are the 'forgotten people' often seemed to be the case once the family had moved away from the refuge. Mothers reported that specialised support for children was more difficult to access and was patchy in its availability. Charmian, as indicated earlier in this chapter, had been able to access a range of support services, while others had faced lengthy referral procedures or a complete lack of service provision. There were further complications if women had to move on again, either for reasons of personal choice or from necessity; support available in one area might not be available in another, with further disruption for the children and possible detrimental consequences.

Counselling for their children was one of the services that women felt was particularly needed, but that was hard to come by. Gemma had tried to obtain this via the National Health Service:

> And I said to the social worker, 'I'd like Anna to have counselling.' And I ended up...I had to go and see the doctor and he had to refer it, and apparently there was a huge long waiting list. And it still wasn't the type of counselling that they need...

Local voluntary agencies had provided a 'listening ear' for two young people; others, as Briony had found, preferred support from within the family:

> We tried to get her [daughter] to go to counselling while we was at [the refuge] but she was having none of it. She said she'd rather talk to me. Which is good that she knows she can come and talk to me. 'Cos not many kids will go and talk to the parents...but she does.

Women very much wanted support and age-related emotional support (not necessarily formal counselling) to be as available for their children as it had been for them and on an equally long-term basis. At the same time, however, their apprehensions regarding statutory services – concerns about being regarded as 'bad' mothers, or having their children taken into care – made approaching these services a difficult option to consider. Workers who had supported them back into the community had been able to offer general advice and assistance in contacting other sources of support, where these were available, but these were limited in number, and information was hard to find. Feedback from refuge workers and other sources indicates that there is a real need for far more community-based services for children and young people. Limited resources for work in the community have, so far, restricted their development, but a growing number of refuge groups and others are now seeking and obtaining funding to set up and maintain projects in this field, and where these are currently available, they are highly valued by participants.[5]

Education

Domestic violence has been shown to have a detrimental effect on children's education: disrupted sleep patterns, lack of a quiet place to study, and general fear and anxiety may make it difficult for them to develop their potential. For some, school may represent a place of safety, whereas others may fear attending; some may want to be at home to protect their mothers who, in turn, may be too distressed to take them to school.

Although coming to the refuge provided a place of safety for the family, it also meant leaving existing schools and friends and starting at a new school, which, as older children were aware, would only be temporary. Once they had been permanently rehoused, children were able to settle into a predictable routine both at home and at school, away from the violence and abuse, and with mothers who were now able to be involved and supportive of what they were doing. In spite of all the setbacks, their mothers were of the opinion that their children had settled in well and made friends. Some women reported initial wariness on the part of teachers, when they realised children had come from a situation of domestic violence and spent time in a refuge – as one mother commented, 'they see "refuge", see "problem"',[6] – but this situation did not appear to have persisted. One of the girls had experienced quite severe bullying that, because of her previous experiences, had caused her to feel revictimised and suicidal. Her mother had not been happy with the school's response to this and had moved her daughter, additionally finding emotional support for her from a local voluntary agency. She was now doing well, both at school and in her social life. This appeared to be true of the majority of the children, which, in turn, had a positive effect on their mothers. As Leanne pointed out, results did not have to be outstanding for her to be happy, as long as her son was enjoying his school life and developing at his own pace:

> Since Christmas he's been totally different and he's got on and…I know he's not going to be a straight A student. But so long as he sticks at school, tries his best and stays out of trouble, that's all I want.

In fact, despite all the difficulties they had encountered, many were doing extremely well academically. Two had already left education and gained professional qualifications; six, who were of an age to think about going on to higher education, were seriously considering university courses. Over half (16), whatever their age, had already given some thought to their future careers. Although these might well change in future years, some choices had been consistently maintained over the period of this study. There were two predominating options among them: the caring professions, where two were already working and another three wanted to join them, or a career in a uniformed service – a branch of the armed forces, police or fire service – which five had selected. Neither stream was gender-exclusive. Speculation on the significance of these choices, if any, is beyond the scope of this book, but may prove an interesting topic for future research.

Contact

Given the destructive effects of domestic violence and abuse on a woman's feelings of self-esteem and confidence, leaving an abusive relationship takes courage and determination. To succeed in building a new life for herself and her children, she needs to feel safe, both physically and mentally. A key element in this is establishing physical and emotional distance between herself and her abuser. Child contact, by bridging this distance, can make recovery more difficult and, for a substantial minority, may provide further opportunity for abuse of both mother and children to take place.[7] Court-mandated contact (as opposed to a genuinely voluntary arrangement) clearly had its problems, and support workers expressed the view that the justice system needed to be far more sensitive to issues around contact where domestic violence was a factor, recalling the physical dangers that contact had created for both mothers and children and the emotional problems women faced in allowing contact.

On the other hand, many women still had some degree of attachment to their former partners, memories of good times with them and their children, and a strong feeling that it was important for children (especially boys) to have an input from their fathers. Provided the children themselves wanted this and would not be in danger, women were prepared to put their own feelings to one side to facilitate contact, as Sylvia explained:

> My son was terribly missing his father, and it was like well...Daniel hasn't done anything, and he idolises his father...I can't in good faith... with my own faith and the loyalty side of me is kind of 'I need to do this for my son. Doesn't matter what my feelings are.' At the end of the day the poor lad's totally surrounded by women all the time, you know. With me and my mum and my sisters and everything...he craves that masculine input.

At the time we first met, seven of the twelve women had child contact arrangements in place: four were court-mandated, three on an informal basis. For two of the women who had made informal arrangements, contact was not a problem; although the first moves had been tricky, relationships were now comparatively amicable and they were able to discuss arrangements and negotiate financial details. Keira put this down to having established her own boundaries and feeling in control:

I had a few problems the first few months, 'cos I didn't want him to know where I lived. And then I thought, 'This is ridiculous', because he is the father of these children. So I started allowing him to come up and pick the children up. And then we went through a bit of a bad patch... I'm not scared of him any longer, Hilary. I know that I can shut that door and I don't have to put up with any more of his rubbish. And now, if I'm truthful, we're quite good friends. And he will come and he will have a meal and we can sit around the table as a family, and he can go away again. And he respects the fact that this is mine not his...this is our domain – mine and the children's. So, yes. I mean I'm painting a rosy picture and making it all sound wonderful, because, [if] I'm really truthful, this is how, at times, it feels.

For Jeannie, however, the informal contact that she had agreed to for the sake of her younger son had initially resulted in a continuation of the abuse:

Like the other day we had a really, really...when I went to pick him [son] up from his house, we had a really, really bad argument and, like, I just thought, I just don't want to...I just don't want to see him any more. I sent him a message on my phone, I said, if you want to see him, I'll just...just meet me somewhere, but I'm not coming anywhere near your house, meet me somewhere and I'll give him to you. And then when you want to bring him back, phone me and I'll come and pick him up. But other than that, I don't want no conversations with him, I just don't. And it brought back a lot of memories. It didn't actually become physical but it could have, and he did threaten me. It was like 'Don't forget what I did to you before', do you know what I mean? And I just thought, 'I just don't need this.' I'm just so glad I wasn't foolish enough to let him know where I live. Even though it's really far, but still...

As she had become stronger and more confident, this abuse had ceased and he was now employing new tactics – 'trying to worm his way back in', as Jeannie put it – but she was having none of it.

Those women who had had court-mandated contact arrangements said that, at first, they had felt fearful of meeting their abuser again and what might happen if they were not 'nice' to him. Lindy had, in fact, been assaulted in front of her children during contact, and the suddenness of the change in his behaviour had left her shocked:

We had a big setback 'cos... Well, in December, I went to meet Damien with the two children, in a hotel. It was all going really, really well, and it turned, and he ended up actually physically assaulting me in front of the children. Yeah.

When she found a new partner, a further crisis occurred, with dramatic pleas to reconsider and start again. Several years down the line, the situation had considerably improved, although she commented that 'he still knows which buttons to press' and that contact was not always easy.

Sylvia had similarly gone through a number of difficult occasions, but had now, by keeping the focus of the meetings firmly on their son, established a system that worked for her.

Even the thought of contact, however, caused a stress reaction in Sally. 'I hate it,' she said, on our second interview. 'I really do hate it. He makes me feel really ill when I see him. The night before, I can't sleep, I feel so ill and that.' A further worry for her was that her current partner (and father of her daughter) might respond to any provocation offered to her during contact, but she had, reluctantly, accepted the court ruling. When, however, she discovered that her son was being physically assaulted during contact, she was determined to take action to protect him. Despite her terror of returning to the locality where the abuse had taken place, and of seeing her former partner, she had appeared in court and successfully challenged both contact and a proposed residence order, and also obtained an injunction to prevent him contacting any member of the family. Her former husband had not broken the injunction, which had now expired. In the meantime, she had moved and was keeping her new address secret, but she was still fearful of being found and of the possible effects on her son.

> I am worried if he finds out where we are, because then Adrian's not going to have the freedom that he's got at the moment. Because he knows that Giles don't know where he lives. But as soon as Giles finds out where we live and he turns up here, Adrian won't want to go outside then.

Court decisions may, at times, place children with their fathers, with mothers needing to arrange for contact and here, too, research has shown that abusive behaviours can be continued.[8] By the time this project ended, Gemma's ex-husband, who had previously had weekend contact with his daughters, had obtained a residence order and was manipulating the arrangements for Gemma to have contact in a way that caused her further distress (for example, by changing times and restricting her to loudspeaker telephone contact). It was clear to her that he was using their children as

a weapon to punish her for leaving, and the thought that the
happen with the younger children, who were in foster care pe
proceedings, was terrifying.

Molly was one of the women who had had no further contact with
their abusive partners; having lost other children into care as a result of
previous relationships, she had every reason to maintain this situation.
Over the time since she left the refuge, she had worked hard to care for
her remaining son, building a good relationship with him and beginning
to establish links with two of her children who were in kinship care. As
a result of her ill-health, this process could not continue and her younger
child was also now in care. She had limited contact with him, but not
with the others, and she was confused and uncertain as to what would
be happening to her children and the extent to which she could now be
involved. An added burden was the way in which this was repeating her
previous losses: 'It really took it out of me...because the others have been
away...the three older ones...my oldest is sixteen next month.' For both
Molly and Gemma, their emotional pain at being separated from their
children was extreme, and the limited periods of contact both precious
and distressing.

Child contact was not, in itself, an issue for the other four women,
since their abusers did not know where they were, and, in two cases,
were serving long prison sentences for other offences. Both Briony and
Charmian, however, shared Sally's concerns that their children might be
harmed or, possibly, abducted. This fear for their children's safety and
the desire to protect them was very real for both, despite having changed
the family name and moved to another part of the country. Charmian's
former partner wanted to see his son and had harassed her family to find
out where she was. 'But he'd be dead in six months going to his dad,' she
commented. Briony's three children, who had no wish to see their father,
had been frightened by the sight of someone who superficially resembled
him:

> The kids got a bit of a fright the other day. They were looking out
> the bedroom window and a bloke walked past and it was the spitting
> image of Gerard. You know, from a distance. Had the same walk,
> the same hair. Everything. And then I saw him one day close up and
> I thought, 'No, it's not.' I knew it wasn't. But the kids saw him for the
> first time the other day and they were 'Uh...uh-huh!'

It is important to recognise that these women were speaking at least four
years after leaving their abuser, but their fears and those of their children

were still in the background of their lives and could, by such chance happenings, be reignited.

Parenting

Being a parent in today's world is not an easy task; once considered purely a private matter, concerns over the health, safety and welfare of children have placed parenting firmly in the public domain as a target for advice, exhortation and criticism. Much of this, either implicitly or explicitly, appears to be directed at mothers, who are still seen as having primary responsibility for the home and child-rearing, and often, it would seem, single mothers are the target.

Women who have experienced domestic violence can be particularly sensitive to any comments, however well-meaning, which might be construed as critical of them in their role as mothers, since this is often an aspect of their lives targeted by their abuser. Accusations of being a 'bad' or 'unfit' mother and threats to have the children removed by Social Services lowered their confidence and self-esteem as mothers and, as previous chapters have shown, instilled feelings of fear and anxiety about any form of statutory intervention. Women also felt guilty about the effect that living in an abusive relationship might be having on their ability as parents and their relationship with their children. Using all their energies to manage the relationship and their own anxieties left them exhausted, making it more difficult to be there for their children, as Gemma commented:

> The thing is, when you've been domestically violently abused…and you have to be focused on not showing any emotions, it's difficult. You end up not showing the love to your children, in a way.

And frequently they needed to impose a level of discipline and restraint on children's activities and behaviour – actions designed to keep them safe, but which might also be perceived as abusive and alienating to the children.[9]

Although the women felt that taking the decision to leave had been by far the best option and that they and their children were much happier as a result, they also regretted having put their children through so much. Lindy felt 'very guilty still. You know, thinking I've put them through that, although it's not all my doing. It's hard.' These feelings were not simply about the abuse and its effects on the whole family, but about having uprooted their children from familiar surroundings and friends, the secrecy necessary while they were in the refuge, and then the need to settle into a new environment, with less ability to provide for them in material terms. Given these feelings of guilt and anxiety, together with their sensitivity around their continuing role as mothers, advice or guidance to women on parenting, to be acceptable, needed to be delivered with care and sensitivity, without being judgemental or patronising.

Arriving at a refuge exhausted, frightened and numb with shock, women needed time and space to begin their own process of recovery, making it more difficult for them to be available emotionally for their children. The support given by children's workers at this time was greatly valued by the majority of the women, who saw their input as twofold: first by working with children as individuals, and then by working with the family as a whole on topics that helped them to move forward and develop together. Women felt comfortable talking to the children's workers about parenting issues in a way that might not have been possible with generalist refuge workers, and they were also able to discuss and learn from their own experiences of being parented, both positive and negative. Specific comments on the sort of help they had been given included workers talking to them about the effects of domestic violence on children, their children's needs and the ways in which these might differ from their own, general child development, and how they could work with their children on talking together, learning to have fun and dealing with specific problems. In her first interview, Molly explained that she had learnt how to talk to her young son:

> She's helped me with his behaviour. When I say, 'Oh, he's driving me…' Don't say it, calm down, talk to him nicely. If you ask him, he'll do it. Well, I've started asking him to do things now and he does it… instead of shouting.

And Leanne felt the advice and help she had been given had been invaluable:

> When I first moved into the ref, I was into working on my relationship with Nigel with them. I was scared he didn't love me any more and… but I knew that wasn't true eventually. Know what I mean? It was just where I had my head at that time.

Given the stress women were under, however, suggestions and offers of parenting support from refuge workers, or any visiting agencies, could be seen as being critical of their efforts. Gemma had responded with an anger born of fear to an approach she felt was judgemental:

It was like…it was just…you know, I was a frightened little rabbit, if you like. Just in a corner constantly ready to kick my feet out and fight.

Some help with parenting issues had been available after leaving the refuge; support from Sure Start and Home-Start had been generally welcomed, and Molly had been able to go to a Mother and Child group run by her son's nursery.

In recent years, the role of good parenting in the lives of children and young people and the need to support parents have been widely recognised; support via the internet, telephone assistance and a range of workshops and courses are now available. A number of these have been specifically designed for parents where domestic violence is an issue within the family. Here, also, the same concerns about sensitivity need to be exercised and any appearance of being judgemental or patronising avoided, if support is to be effective.

The changing family

No family stays static for ever; children grow older and leave home, new members are born, new relationships develop, old ones disintegrate. A study of this length is bound to encounter and reflect at least some of these changes, all of which impact on dynamics within the family. For most of the families in the project, the most significant changes had been the natural development of their children. By the time we last met, preschoolers were in primary education, others had moved on to secondary schools, and the five eldest were now young adults. Two of these had already left to pursue independent lives; others, and some of the older adolescents, were thinking about leaving to go to university. These changes, although they represented further losses, were welcomed and seen as positive aspects of women's lives.

And there were significant inward movements as well: the new partnerships described in Chapter 4 had added another adult to three households, and two of them brought with them children from previous relationships. Sally had been joined by the father of her daughter and one of his three children, with the other two visiting each weekend. Her daughter was delighted to be with her father, and Sally's son was pleased to have playmates of his own age. Liz was visited regularly by both the children of her new partner; her two children, who had been vociferous in their dislike of an earlier partner, approved of the new relationship and welcomed the visits from his children, who were much younger than them. John was the only new partner who had never been a parent and he had found the adjustment difficult. Lindy appreciated what he was going through and felt that things were moving in the right direction for all of them:

> We do have problems occasionally and it's the children. But I can understand that because he's taken on...you know, he's got a hell of a lot of baggage. And he's got no children of his own so...at the moment...he says, 'Lindy, it gets me down.' I say, 'It gets me down too!' That's children, isn't it? Just want to get in your car and drive away occasionally, but you can't. I think at the moment, they're damned hard work. That's just normal children. They're always bickering and fighting and answering back. I think that's normal. So we're all still learning to live with each other. We're getting there gradually.

Lindy's comments on learning to live with each other resonated with views expressed by the other women with changes to their households. None of these relationships had been the result of a sudden decision; they had developed over a period of time, giving everyone the opportunity to get to know each other and adjust to the new situation. All of the women had lived with the insecurity of domestic violence and abuse for many years and had gone through a period of immense change when they decided to leave. Now, at least for the majority of them, it appeared that family lives and relationships had been rebuilt to the extent that change could be accepted and accommodated as part of their lives.

A new picture

The focus of this project was on women as individuals, rather than in their roles as partners or mothers, and their children were not directly interviewed. Nevertheless, they were often around before and after the interviews (and sometimes during, when domestic needs took priority). Over the years, I saw many changes in their behaviour. Children who had been shy and withdrawn were more confident, angry and aggressive behaviour was replaced by a pleasant social interaction with someone who was a stranger to them, school friends played with them in the house and garden, and there was altogether a different feeling within the home. Their mothers talked of how family life had changed after leaving the abusive relationship. Leanne's son felt safe to be untidy:

And I've seen such a change in Nigel. It's like he used to count all his toys and make sure everything was still there. And...he loves it, he can leave anything everywhere and he knows it'll still be there when he comes back, nobody's sold it. Brilliant.

For Sally, it was the different atmosphere in the home:

It is nice now because we can...we can laugh and we can joke and we can play about without being ...getting told to 'Shut up all of you' and 'I'm trying to do this' or 'I want to sleep'. So...

And one of the young people, Lindy's teenage daughter, Rose, asked me directly to pass on a message to other children,[10] showing how she felt about her new life: 'I want the children to know it all comes right in the end.'

Finally, from a second interview, a defining image of how families had learnt new and satisfying ways of being together: Sally, with her son and daughter either side of her, swinging their linked hands and skipping down the pavement, laughing.

Summary

- Children are aware of violence within the home from an early age, even when mothers think they are concealing the abuse, and are affected by it in a variety of ways. Clear links exist between domestic violence and the likelihood of child abuse.

- After leaving the abusive situation, children may feel more able to show their feelings of distress and fear and the sadness and anger at all they have lost This may result in the emergence of a wide range of difficult behaviours and emotional problems, with some children being more adversely affected than others.

- The support provided in refuges for children and young people was seen as valuable in providing a safe and supportive environment for them to meet others with similar experiences, talk to workers if they wished, and generally relax in a space that was specifically for them. This, in turn, had a positive effect on mothers.

- Refuge services for young children were generally considered to be excellent, but women wanted more support and resources within the refuge for older children.

- Women wanted age-related support and services to be available for children and young people on a long-term basis after leaving the refuge, but found that provision was extremely limited and hard to access. There was a real need for community-based support and professional services to be available across the country.

- Being away from the violence and in a safe and predictable routine had a very positive effect on children and young people. Their mothers were extremely proud of the way they had adapted to the new environment, with improvements, over time, in their emotional and behavioural difficulties and their educational progress.

- Where their children wanted it, and were not in danger, women put aside their own feelings to facilitate contact with their fathers. Although some were able to manage this relationship amicably, for others it was an occasion for further abuse to take place.

- Women who had no contact with their abuser were still nervous of being found and fearful for their safety and that of their children. These feelings were still in evidence several years after leaving the relationship.

- The women's ability to parent had often been affected by the domestic violence, with their role as mothers being undermined by their abuser. They felt guilty at how their children had suffered and anxious about the effect on their relationship. Given these feelings, advice and guidance on parenting needed to be delivered with care and sensitivity.

- Their children were a central focus in the lives of the women, giving them the determination and motivation to build a new life for the family. Drawing on their own inner resources and the support they had received had enabled the majority of families to find new and satisfying ways of being together.

Notes

1. The findings in this chapter reflect those of larger studies involving both mothers and children (Hague et al.1996; Hester and Pearson 1998; McGee 2000a; Mullender et al. 2002; Radford and Hester 2006). Individual notes will be inserted for other references and where specific points occur in a study. An overview and

commentary on a wide range of research into children and domestic violence can be found in Hester, Pearson and Harwin with Abrahams (2007).

2. In 90 per cent of reported incidents, children have been in the same or an adjacent room when the abuse took place (Abrahams 1994; Stark and Flitcraft 1996).

3. It has been suggested (Hague *et al.* 1996; Mullender *et al.* 2002) that older children may show fewer behavioural problems as they have greater ability to make sense of what is happening and resources to protect themselves. Any problems, however, may be more deep-rooted and harder to resolve. Resilience may be a factor that enables some individuals to deal with, or recover from, the impact of circumstances where they are at risk, including domestic violence, more quickly than others (Jaffe, Wolfe and Wilson 1990; Radford and Hester 2006). Radford and Hester point out that a wide range of mediating factors, including age, gender and the availability of support, may be involved in creating resilience, and that these will vary from child to child.

4. Despite worrying concerns that many children and young people think domestic violence is acceptable in certain circumstances (McCarry 2009), evidence for the intergenerational transmission of violence appears contradictory and not generally supportive of this theory.

5. Humphreys and Thiara 2002; Supporting People 2007. NSPCC reports (Allnock *et al.* 2009; Stanley *et al.* 2009) comment that there is a general shortage of services for children and young people and, in particular, a lack of services for those who have suffered sexual abuse.

6. Hague *et al.* (1996) found similar concerns among teachers regarding 'refuge' children.

7. Humphreys and Thiara 2002; Povey *et al.* 2008; Radford and Hester 2006; Saunders with Barron 2003; Saunders 2004.

8. Radford and Hester 2006; Saunders with Barron 2003.

9. Similar findings on the impact of domestic violence on parenting come from Damant *et al.* (2009), Lapierre (2008), Mullender *et al.* (2002), Radford and Hester (2006) and Sanderson (2008). These studies also indicate that mother/ child relationships will often show considerable improvement once they are out of the abusive situation, and that sensitive support and help can assist women to work through these difficulties and further enhance the relationship.

10. The children and young people in Mullender *et al.* (2002) similarly sent messages for other children. They are practical, passionate and deeply moving.

Chapter 8

The View from Here

The women who chose to take part in this study gave a variety of reasons for responding to my invitation. First, it was a time for them – a space in which to reflect on their individual journeys. For most, it was also a celebration of their new lives and achievements with someone who had met them at a low point in their lives and was able to recognise how far they had come. And finally, there was the realisation that their experiences, thoughts and opinions were considered to be worth listening to and could be used to help other women.[1] The long-term nature of the research added to these ideas; it meant that women were able to talk not only about their time in the refuge and what this had meant to them, but also about the long-term effects of abuse and the struggle to build a new life. Jeannie brought all this together very clearly:

> Because I thought, well, someone's listening to me. And if it's going to help someone else, then why not? Because it helps people…I mean, it's not just in the refuge, it's a few years down the line.

In recognising the value that their knowledge and experience could have for others, women saw the need for honesty in their self-appraisal; they were prepared to talk, not only about the positive aspects and the successes, but about the choices and dilemmas they faced, the moments of self-doubt and despair, and where they had found the strength to continue.

Every meeting revealed new changes in the women's lives, new challenges and opportunities emerging and new facets of their experience to discuss. To try to capture as much of this as possible, each session gave time for the women to reflect on both recent and past events, and talk about what they felt were currently the important issues for them. Every interview marked a stage in their evolving lives, but, at our last meeting, we worked together on looking back over all the years since they had taken the decision to leave. Reflecting on change over this longer period showed more clearly how their lives had altered and enabled the women to explore how they themselves had changed and to speculate on what had been significant in facilitating those changes.

From their voices has come, for the first time, a rich and intricate picture of life many years after leaving, of how women go about recovering from their experiences, and what helps or hinders the process of rebuilding their lives.

A new way of being

Meeting over a period of years and with long intervals between each visit, I was vividly aware of how the women had changed, both mentally and physically. Their appearance altered – they wore brighter colours, took more care of themselves and their appearance, and they moved with greater confidence and assurance. (These changes were also the indicators that workers identified as showing that women were beginning to move on from the experience of abuse.) And how the women spoke about themselves changed as well, with a growing sense that they were individuals with their own identity, their own values and a sense of their personal worth. Although fear and anxiety were still, for some of them, present in the background of their lives, this was not something they routinely dwelt on, nor did it affect their generally positive view of life. Even in the adverse situations experienced by Jeannie and Gemma, there seemed to be an active engagement with life and a desire to make headway. Alone among the women, Molly had not been able to sustain this growth of ability; on an upward trend for a long time, her overwhelming health problems had meant that she had been unable to make further progress.

My perceptions of this personal growth were borne out by what the women said about themselves. They knew just how much they had changed, and, to them, the most significant element had been the growth of an inner strength – an awareness of their own power. Often, it had been other people who first recognised and pointed out this change to them. For Lindy, it had been her abusive former partner, and she relished the moment:

> And actually Damien turned round and he said to me, 'You're strong.' That would have been last year. 'Cos it took me aback. I was like, 'What?' He says, 'You're one of the strongest people I will ever meet in this world.' I was like 'Wow!' Then I felt like going 'Na na, na na na.'

Linked to this idea of emotional strength was the other word women used to describe how they had changed: determined. This characteristic had, in fact, been evident during the abusive relationship, in the tenacious way they clung on to survival and tried to protect themselves and their children, but now it was a positive upward force – a drive to get things done, to achieve something in their lives. Liz explained how determination had played a major role in her progress: 'I wanted to do summat for me. I were determined, because me mam thought I'd never come to much.'

These feelings of strength and determination sprang from their growing sense of personal worth and self-respect. Proving to themselves, as well as to their abuser, and those who had underrated them in the past, that they could be strong and independent further boosted their confidence and self-esteem, replacing the negative self-images they had internalised with a more positive view of themselves.[2] The women recognised that they were now the ones who were in control of their lives and able to take responsibility for their actions. And valuing themselves meant that they were clear about how they expected to be treated and were able to set boundaries for themselves and others. As Sally's current partner, who had known her for many years, commented, 'You know when to say "No" now. You never used to be like that.' This new sense of personal integrity was particularly noticeable when women talked of the possibility of new partners. They were, as Chapter 4 showed, extremely wary of taking this step and adamant that future relationships needed to work on a basis of mutual respect. Lindy had made it clear from the outset that her new relationship was to be based on love, not dependency:

> That's one thing I say to John…and I still do…this is awful really… 'Just remember I don't *need* you, I *want* to be with you. Yeah. 'Cos I don't *need* you for anything.' Just be independent again and not be sort of tied to someone, that is nice. 'Cos although we're together, I mean, now it's different.

These changes in attitude and outlook were not sudden – they had developed over a long period and often women were surprised to look back and realise quite how different they had become. Nor had the process been an easy one; indeed, in some ways, being strong and independent made life more difficult and exhausting as they wrestled with new problems and learnt new skills. Becoming proactive and assertive after years of subjugation was, in itself, a hard task, and it was even more of a struggle when new attitudes and relationships had to be developed and maintained with friends, family and former partners.

Women saw rebuilding their lives, both in practical and emotional terms, as a continuing process: they still had problems in their lives; they still had days when past experiences revived old pain and losses. But they had made progress, they had achieved things; they were, as they said, 'getting there'. Sylvia explored how these contrasts played out in her life:

> But you have looked after yourself now, you know, you've got your weight off, you're going to the gym, you've got active, you've got involved in the scouting again, you've got involved with the church mission and all the things that I would have done 15 years ago without batting an eyelid, you know. So I kind of brought myself full circle. But it hasn't been easy and I wouldn't say that every day is a success – that would be a lie. There are days... But they're less and less and more cope-able. So I suppose it's just...an ongoing project is how I look at it, every day is different.

These positive, but realistic, views of their circumstances were apparent in all of the final interviews (except, for obvious reasons, that with Molly). But what had happened to create this change in their outlook?

Realignment

In earlier research, I had seen the beginnings of similar changes in a small number of women who had left abusive relationships and had spent time in a refuge. In general, they had either recently left the refuge or were coming to the end of their stay there. I used the term 'realignment' to identify this changed perception of themselves and their role in society.[3] Two of the women from this small group (Charmian and Liz) joined the current project. (Leanne was also a member of the original study, but, at that time, had only recently come to the refuge and was still coming to terms with her situation.) It was exciting to see how far these women had come in their journeys since we first met, but also to see the way in which, to a greater or lesser extent, these changes were now taking place for all of the women.

Although they knew that they had changed and could identify their new strengths, the women were unsure about how this had happened or what exactly had occurred. Lindy was typical in her response:

> No, I don't know, where my...where does my strength come from? I think it's...um...determination. I sometimes...I think I sat down in the past and go to myself, 'I'll show you all.' But it does, you do find it... I

don't know where it comes from, something just appears, I think. If I could bottle it, I'd sell it. Yeah!

Twelve very different women, each with their own personality and background, and different pathways from an abusive relationship to independent living – but in looking together at what had influenced them as they built their new lives, comments that had been scattered throughout their narratives began to come together. From these, it was possible to begin to identify factors common to all of them and that, in retrospect, had contributed to this process of change. The starting point, in each case, had been the refuge and the services it provided.

The refuge

Asking what had been the single most important factor about the refuge produced a unanimous answer: safety. It had been, quite literally, for the majority of the women, a lifesaver. Seven out of the twelve felt that, but for the existence of refuges, they would now be dead. 'When I think of it,' said Jeannie, 'that's the truth, I'd be dead.' Some had already tried, or considered, killing themselves, driven by their own feelings of being unworthy to live, or feeling unable to endure the abuse any longer. Others were certain that they would have been killed by their abusers, either because physical violence had gone too far or because death threats would have been carried out. Nor were these concerns limited only to their own safety – Briony had feared for the lives of her three children as well as for herself:

> Oh, I know exactly what would have happened. The threats to kill me, he would have carried them out. It would have been either all of us, or specially me, or Ellie, seriously hurt…and he would have done. Well, he did when he put a scar on my neck.

This was no Victorian melodrama; this was real life. Many of these women had previously been hospitalised as a result of physical violence and their legitimate fears are borne out by official statistics.[4]

Feeling physically safe and secure meant that they no longer needed to be continually 'on edge', waiting for the next incident of abuse, but never certain what it would be or when it would happen. Feelings of mental safety developed more gradually, as women began to trust those around them and realise that they were not being judged or condemned. A key element in this was the realisation that all the other residents had been subjected to domestic violence and abuse; that they were not, as they had believed and been told, alone in their suffering. Isolation from any social contact, apart from that of their abuser, was replaced by a group of their peers, with whom they could share their stories and both give and receive support. And being with others who understood and accepted the reality of their experience meant that there was no longer any need for secrecy or to explain and justify their actions. This openness and support was vital to changing their outlook, as Keira explained:

> It was almost like a self-help therapy that we went through. It was the camaraderie of us all getting together and us all…and it was that that helped me get through, it wasn't just [the refuge], it was the friendship that I'd made in there, because I no longer needed to pretend. I could say, 'Hey, I'm Keira, this is what's happened to me, I need help.' And I got it through the friendship that I'd made. I didn't need to pretend any longer, I didn't need to say to people, 'Well, this is what's happened' – we're all in the same boat.

Equally important in recovering from the abuse was the input and attitude of the workers and volunteers within the refuge. They described their approach as one of respect, treating women as responsible individuals who most clearly understood their own position and, given information and support, were best placed to make decisions about their own futures.[5] Often, this attitude was not easy for women to understand, since this was not how they had been treated by their abusers, nor, in some cases, by the agencies they had dealt with in the past.

Learning to take responsibility, sometimes for the first time in their lives, was not easy, and this was also the time when women began to realise all that they had lost and the reality of the problems that lay ahead. Workers were aware that this was sometimes the moment when women might choose to go back to their abuser. As Lindy explained, it was the input of her refuge worker that had enabled her to stay away at this crucial moment:

> She deserved a medal. She was that…at the time I looked back and think, 'Oh, for God's sake, will you shut up, I don't want to hear that', but she'd be saying, 'It's going to be all right.' But in that heat of the moment it's not all right. 'I want to go home now.' You know, you just want to get off, turn it all round. Go back…and I'll be honest, at times I would have been tempted to go back to Damien just to get out of there. But what kept me going, I don't know, but Lydia [worker] was there every morning to say, 'Are you all right?'

Even without these personal internal struggles, the close proximity of residents to each other and the inevitable tensions of refuge life were bound to cause some difficulties. All of the women and their children were under considerable emotional stress; sharing with women who had different standards of hygiene and ways of dealing with their children could be difficult, and conforming to necessary rules and regulations could be irksome. Sometimes women's expectations of the support they felt they needed were not met – workers themselves were frequently under pressure and might not respond appropriately, or have the time they would have liked to devote to each individual woman.

Nevertheless, the women emphasised that their comments in no way detracted from the value that they placed on these services and what they had meant to them. Many talked of the refuge where I first met them as having marked a turning point. It had given them space and time to think about their lives and all that had happened, and a sense of direction, acting as a launching pad into a new life. 'It gave me the ten weeks that I needed,' Keira said, 'to sit back, to reflect on everything that was being done and take a completely different course in my life.' Liz, who, like others, had left refuges to return to her abusive relationship on previous occasions, recognised how much their continued support and acceptance had meant to her: 'I wouldn't be as happy as I am if it wasn't for them giving me a chance and being there for me.' And Leanne marked the anniversary of the day she first came to the refuge, every year, with a small private celebration:

> Every year, on the fourth of December, it's another year. That's the day I come to the refuge. I celebrate. Even if it's just having a drink, or summat like that, or just anything. It's just I done another year.

From their arrival, feeling worthless and exhausted, the experience of living in a community that accepted and valued them as they were without judging them, being listened to and supported, gradually began to restore their confidence and sense of personal worth. The shock of leaving and of understanding all they had lost had started to be assimilated, and they were beginning to access their own inner resources. Briony reflected that, 'At the end of the day, you come out a lot stronger than what you were originally'. Nevertheless, as discussed in Chapter 1, 'going out' was daunting, as well as exciting; women were concerned about how they would manage on their own and fearful for their safety and that of their children. Making a successful transition depended on three interlinking factors: appropriate housing, continued support and building their own network of supportive relationships.

Life after leaving

For women who have experienced domestic violence and abuse, the importance of being able to access permanent, good quality accommodation, which is appropriate to their needs, cannot be overestimated. Not only does it give women a sense of physical and mental safety, allaying one of their major concerns, it strengthens feelings of being worthy of having decent housing and enables them to start building up a home and a predictable routine for the family. For the women in this study, having a secure base of this nature gave them a sense of stability, making it easier to work on other problems in their lives and to continue their recovery from the effects of abuse. Where this had not been possible, or the process had been interrupted, as it had been for Jeannie and Gemma, it had proved far more difficult to remain positive and determined. Although they were trying to keep going, life remained unpredictable and the anxiety of not knowing when they would be required to move on made it difficult to engage with their other problems. Not only did the temporary nature of their accommodation make it difficult to make and sustain a relationship with just one support worker, there seemed little point in trying to make friends in the community around them.

Together with finding a permanent place to live and regard as their home, women rated the continuing availability of support from the refuge group to be of equal importance in the success of their new lives. Although their stay in the refuge had started to build up the strengths that they needed to sustain a tenancy and live independently, for most of them these feelings were still quite fragile. Now they were about to be tested outside the safety of the refuge, in a world that had, in the past, appeared, at best, to be indifferent to them and, at worst, actively hostile. Having a support worker, whom they knew and trusted, alongside them as they assimilated the skills of independent living, tackled problems and learnt to be their own advocate, made this process much easier. For the few where this had not been available, or where, for whatever reason, it had not been able to continue, the transition was felt to have been more difficult. As in the refuge, workers aimed to encourage, offer choices and options and challenge women to step outside their comfort zone, but support them while they did so. Support needed to be robust, reliable and flexible, gradually becoming less as the woman gained in confidence, but accessible if circumstances should change.

THE VIEW FROM HERE / 153

And as they moved away and into their new lives, women needed to build their own sustaining support network. Restoring their links to the wider community and the freedom to talk to others was a welcome change after the restrictions that had previously been placed on them. It was also important in enabling them to continue to live independently since, as Gemma's story shows, repetition of the loneliness and isolation they had experienced during the original abusive relationship could drive them back to their abuser or into new and unhelpful relationships. Positive sources of support, on the other hand, from family, friends in the new community and, for some, new and non-violent relationships, reinforced women's sense of belief in themselves and their abilities and constituted a support network they could rely on. In building these relationships, the most difficult issue for women was that of trust. The loss of trust in others that had resulted from the abuse, together with concerns as to how those around them would react to them, was a constant theme in our discussions. While the refuge had provided a safe place to talk, leaving created a situation where they were again uncertain as to whom to trust and what others in the community would think of them if they talked about their experiences.

As the women gained in confidence, they were better able to judge who they would talk to and what they could talk about, and, as they developed their new lives, they were looking forward, rather than back. Nevertheless, there were still times when they wanted the support of those who knew where they were coming from and to whom they did not need to explain themselves. Interestingly, it became apparent that taking part in the research interviews was, in itself, a validating and positive process. Sylvia explained:

It was, I suppose, another rung on the ladder of confidence climbed. Being interviewed about it all is quite hard at first, but, in an odd way, both the refuge and the interviews all add to the steps forward – and if it helps other women to take a stand, it has my thumbs up!

Being able to talk freely, within a supportive environment, has been recognised as having considerable therapeutic value[6] in a wide range of settings; helplines, drop-in centres and support groups can play an important role in this respect, providing continuing support and helping women at times when they feel particularly vulnerable.

Rebuilding a life

Inner strength and determination, springing from a sense of their own identity and personal values – these were the qualities that women recognised as having grown within them over the years since they had left the abusive relationship. Within a very disparate group of women, feelings of safety and being accepted and supported within a community appeared to be the common factors facilitating these developments and enabling women to change their perceptions of themselves and mobilise their own resources to rebuild their lives.

To understand this process in more detail, we need to look again at the way the structure of women's lives had previously imploded under the impact of domestic violence and abuse. Women explained, in Chapter 1, how criticism and derogatory comments had eaten away at their self-esteem and confidence, how their abusers had come to control their entire world, isolating them from the community around them, and how they had lived in a permanent state of fear and apprehension. I used Maslow's concept of human needs (Figure 1.1, page 23) to suggest that these effects can be seen as a gradual demolition of their status as individuals with a place in society. The succession of losses imposed by the abuse – loss of personal worth, of links to others, of physical and mental safety – slowly reduced their lives to the basic needs for survival, and, at times, even this was at risk. But even at this low ebb, fearful and constrained as they were, women were doing what they could to protect themselves and their children. Eventually, for whatever reason, they found the strength to leave. Through listening to their stories, it has been possible to trace the way in which women began the process of rebuilding their lives and the factors that helped this.

For all of them, safety, first within the refuge and subsequently in their new communities, was the primary requirement. Apart from the basic needs to sustain life, it was, as Maslow identified and refuge workers know, the foundation without which no further steps can be taken.[7] Finding themselves in an accepting and supportive community ended their isolation and began the process of rebuilding their confidence and sense of personal worth. Being able to take this support with them as they started their new lives sustained this level of achievement while they developed their own support network and capabilities. Each achievement, however small, boosted their self-esteem, and as they began to feel accepted within their new communities, they reached a point where they were independent, able to act for themselves and decide what they wanted for their futures.

Because of the clarity and honesty of the women's accounts, we can begin to understand how difficult the process had been and to identify the 'pinch points' where this growth might halt or go into reverse: an unsafe or unstable environment and the lack of a support network or a listening ear at a critical moment when they felt particularly isolated or vulnerable. These were the moments when women might consider returning to their abuser (as had happened in the past) or starting new and potentially unhelpful relationships or coping strategies. Conversely, we can learn about the strengths that women drew on at these points: the availability of ongoing support, the knowledge that they had been strong enough to leave and that, whatever the future held, there were people they could trust to help them. A further factor that emerged as important to women was *by whom* these services should be provided.

feminism –
feminist
theory ?.

Women for women services?

The services that these women accessed while in the refuge were women only, and this was also true of the support they received from the refuge group after being rehoused. Services from other agencies might be provided by male or female staff and professionals, and women were unlikely to be offered a choice. I wondered how the women themselves felt about this. Had the availability of women-only services been a factor in their recovery? Had they wanted services for women provided by women? Did they want a choice within agencies as to whom they could deal with?[8]

Although 80 per cent of the women (ten out of the twelve) were emphatically in favour of women for women services, none of them rushed straight into giving a snap judgement on this issue. Most went on to raise a number of interesting issues around service provision within this concept. There was a general view that, for women who had suffered or were suffering domestic violence and abuse, specialist services provided by women for women were essential. This included the greater availability of drop-in and advice centres, as well as refuge and outreach provision. For most of them, when they first came to the refuge, men were seen as a continuing threat to their safety. They had just left situations of violence and abuse, generally perpetrated by men; their emotions were all over the place, and they were in a state of shock. Bringing a man into this situation, as Leanne explained, was likely to cause an immediate and terrified reaction:

> Well, if a woman's just been beaten up by a man, the last thing she wants to be surrounded by is men. I'm not being funny but…I mean they're all going through that, they're all going to…I know what it's like. You can snap at the slightest thing and it's… I know a lot of the women found…'cos they actually had a handyman [in the refuge]… and one or two of the women, specially the ones when I was actually working there, were very wary of a man. Not of him, once they got to know him, but that initial 'There's a man in the house'. It's like, 'Whoa', back against the wall, sort of thing, back away. And you can see it in their eyes sometimes, and it's like… I mean, fair enough, he's harmless, he wouldn't hurt a fly, but you don't know that, do you? And it's like when workmen come in as well, a lot of the women scattered to the bedrooms.

She and several other women also felt that similar considerations might well apply to men who experience violence and abuse, and that here, too, specialist services might be preferred.

There was, however, a general recognition that it was not simply gender that was significant in service provision. Being a woman was not necessarily the best or indeed the only qualification for the job; attitude was equally important. Gemma, whose complex problems have been discussed earlier, felt that women had been harder on her than men would have been and was one of the two who did not want women-only services. Keira and Sylvia fully supported women-only services, but emphasised the importance of attitude. Sylvia phrased her answer with care:

> It wouldn't bother me to speak to a male, if it was a male that was in touch with his feminine side, I think is the thing. Now the probation officer that was dealing with Miles [ex-partner]… now him, I could have talked to him about anything, totally at ease with him. So no, I would see a man or a woman…because even with women there's some that I don't feel I could talk to. So I think it's not gender as in persona, you know, [it's] how they walk in and make you feel. They need to be very in tune that they're walking in to someone that's probably been through the most horrendous time of their life. And I just do think it is not so much…I mean, I don't know how other women feel, but I personally…it wasn't about gender, it was about how they made me feel. I didn't want a man that came in, that was quite stern, 'cos instantly it was like 'Right, now I'm this way again, I'm guarded again' – you know what I mean, I'm being careful – is he a threat? Whereas another man come in and he'd be so friendly and 'How are you?' Tone, everything was in tone, you know.

Keira argued, as well, for a balance between academic and practical knowledge in providing front-line services. In her view, women who had experienced domestic violence and abuse, provided that they had gone a long way down the road to full recovery, might well be able to offer a better understanding of problems:

> I think that there should be a fair balance in terms of...I'm not saying that someone that's been to college or been to university, learnt a lot out of a book, is not as good as someone that's actually experienced it. But what I'm saying is there should be a balance between the two. Uh...I do feel that if you have experienced domestic violence, and you have been into a refuge, you have a far better broad spectrum outlook on exactly what the hell it's like. And if your life has been turned completely upside down, you have an even better [one]. Now that sounds terrible but it's how I feel.

The benefits that personal experience could bring to helping others was also something Lindy commented on:

> I think...do you know, like a midwife who's helping a woman have a baby? Until she's had one herself, 'Don't tell me what to do, 'cos you don't know.' I think it...I think it'd be helpful. I have been there, yeah.

Although the consensus was firmly in favour of women-only spaces, Lindy, who had felt 'Don't bring a man near me!' when she first came to the refuge, was one of a number who commented on the benefits that children could gain from having positive male role models, although she appreciated that there could be risks involved:

> I think it would have been a positive experience, more so when children have positive male role models around. Because it is very women-oriented. And...more so for the children, because their vision on men...it's a dodgy one because I think women can become quite attached to a positive role model! But to have them there, and dealing with some things, yeah, I think it would be helpful. Perhaps a male child worker. Just...just to have that positiveness, rather than that all men are bastards – they're not.

Liz, the only other woman who was not in favour of women-only services, felt that segregation could be counter-productive and that women needed to see that not all men were potential abusers:

> I mean, I know it can have lots of problems having men working, but, you know, not all men are bad. And I think it makes women more

hungry to go out and get a man, because there's no men to be seen, it's all females. From my point of view and...I do honestly think that men – straight, gay, whatever – should be able to have their input to convince women that not everybody's bad. You know, give men a chance to say, 'Look, you know, all right, you've come across a bad 'un but ...' – I just think it just segregates them a little bit and maybe that's why they rebel and go out and sleep about and shack up wi' t'first man what comes along, because it's been women only. It's like when you're dieting – you tell yourself you can't have chocolate cake, you want it more. And then you go have it and binge. It's just exactly the same.

The concept of 'going wild' in this way, identified in earlier research,[9] may have more to do with the reaction to the sudden freedom to enjoy previously restricted activities and also test the boundaries of acceptable behaviour, rather than purely to being in a segregated environment. It can also be a way of avoiding the need to deal with emerging feelings of pain and grief. In considering women's actions after leaving the refuge, these can, perhaps, rather be seen as a response to the moments of isolation and vulnerability discussed earlier in this chapter. Missing the cuddles and closeness that could exist even in an abusive relationship and the fear that they might not have the strength and determination to live without another adult can, as Chapter 4 indicated, be precipitating factors in starting new relationships. Nevertheless, Liz's thoughts offer a different and interesting perspective on the role of non-violent men in confronting abusive behaviour.

This is clearly a difficult and sensitive area for service providers to assess. In the early days of services for women escaping domestic violence, a few refuges did, in fact, employ anti-sexist male workers to offer non-violent role models,[10] before becoming women-only in the 1970s. This is still the case in refuges in some areas, where male children's workers are seen as a positive influence. However, from their own experience and from talking to other refuge residents, these women felt that, at least when they were at their most vulnerable, they and the others they had met wanted women-only services, which focused on their needs and provided spaces where they were safe, free to talk and make choices, and begin to feel empowered before facing men again. Quite simply, most women who had experienced domestic violence and abuse did not feel safe with men around and, from their accounts, the provision of services for women by women was a significant factor in the development of their confidence and self-esteem.

As regards support from other agencies after leaving the refuge, women were already apprehensive about dealing on their own with agencies and would have liked the option of talking to female members of staff, especially if they were without the support of the refuge worker. Although, as indicated in Chapter 3, there had been individual members of staff, both male and female, who had gone out of their way to be helpful, several of them had encountered male agency staff who were obstructive, actively hostile, or uncomprehending of their problems. Briony felt that some women might well be able to deal with this, but that a female member of staff might be more understanding of their position:

> 'Cos I don't really think that a woman who's gone through, say, severe domestic violence is going to end up sitting across a table from a bloke. So I think it's definitely got to be women-orientated. So just to be able for the person to be able to relax. So...because from my experience I know such women tend to talk to women better than they do if it was a man. I mean, I still find it hard to have a full-blown conversation with a man. You know, if a woman is strong, then she can actually get on with it. But there's a lot of very vulnerable people, and I think they would feel better talking, I think, with a woman, face to face.

Staffing and resource implications might make this option difficult to implement, and it was clear that, over time, women, although still wary, did find a greater ease in their dealings with male workers. As existing agency policies on domestic violence and abuse become an accepted and automatic part of practice, this situation should improve, but this still appears to be some way off.

Conclusion

Building and sustaining a new life after leaving an abusive relationship is not easy, as the individual stories of these women have shown. There are material problems to overcome: poor housing, poverty and debt, opportunities for education or employment, and concerns for their children. And there are emotional barriers to break: becoming able to trust again, to reach out to others, to rebuild personal integrity, and to learn to live again. This is not neat, simple or straightforward; the effects that domestic violence and abuse had had on them were evident long after they had left the relationship, with moments of insecurity, self-doubt, the fear of retribution, and memories and feelings about the abuse. These women, like most of us, made mistakes, went down blind alleys, felt dispirited, and some were still struggling under adverse circumstances. But even when things were not looking good for them, they had developed an inner strength and determination and were able to see the way ahead in a positive light. As Lindy commented, 'I'm not scared of anything now. It's made me find myself, what I want and what I don't want. ...I'm the boss.'

The climate within which this personal growth could develop and the factors that supported it emerged clearly from the interviews, with the baseline being the establishment of a sense of physical and mental safety, first in the refuge and then in their new locations. The next step was to link themselves back into a social and supportive network: a task initially easier to accomplish within the refuge, where social skills could re-emerge that would assist them as they moved into their new communities. And both within the refuge and beyond it, there were sources of support that fostered their growing sense of self-esteem and confidence, enabling them to recognise the inner resources that had helped them to survive, and channel them into building a new life. Using Maslow's concepts, most of them now felt reasonably safe; they belonged to a community and possessed a growing sense of their worth as individuals. True, as Maslow had argued, they were still held back by social and economic barriers, but the constraints imposed by memories of their past experiences were gradually fading, as they proved to themselves and others, that they were full and worthy members of society. It was at this point that many of them chose to widen their horizons and look to a new future.

Summary

- In the years after leaving the abusive relationship, women in this study had developed a sense of their own personal worth, inner strength and a determination to achieve something in their lives. They felt in control of their lives and able to take responsibility for their actions.

- In valuing themselves, they were clear about how they expected to be treated and were able to set boundaries for themselves and others. This was particularly in evidence when discussing the possibility of new intimate partnerships.

- Developing these new strengths was not easy after years of abuse, and the women recognised that rebuilding their lives would be an ongoing process.

- The factors that were key to developing this changed perspective were a sense of physical and mental safety and the existence of an accepting and supportive community. This process began in the refuge, where peer support was able to end their isolation and they could be helped to channel the inner resources that had helped them to survive into building a new life.

- Making a successful transition from the refuge to independent living was related to three interlinking factors: appropriate housing, continuing support and building a network of supportive relationships.

- Women's feelings of confidence and self-esteem could be fragile at times and the long-term availability of support of a less intensive nature was an important consideration for them.

- The majority of women wanted women-only services to be available for women who have experienced domestic violence and abuse. Attitude and a balance of practical and academic knowledge were also factors that needed to be taken into account in service provision.

- It was felt that the employment of non-violent male children's workers could be beneficial in providing role models for children.

Notes

1. Similar reasons for participating have been registered by other researchers (Hoff 1990; Humphreys and Thiara 2002; Kirkwood 1993; Women's Budget Group 2008). As Humphreys and Thiara comment, these voices form a potentially valuable, but underused resource.

2. The possibility of positive growth after a traumatic experience has been identified in other research (Humphreys and Joseph 2004; Radford and Hester 2006; Sanderson 2008; Tischler, Edwards and Vostanis 2009).

3. Abrahams 2007. The other women interviewed for this study originally took part in research carried out for the Department of Communities and Local Government (Supporting People 2007).

4. The statistics on women killed by their partners or ex-partners, although falling slightly from the two a week recorded for many years, are still high (Povey et al. 2009). Chapter 7 examined the continuing risks to children, where domestic violence and abuse was a factor.

5. This model of support characterised the work of the earliest refuges. The way in which this support can lead to a changed attitude among women has been identified in previous research (Abrahams 2007; Clifton 1985; Dobash and Dobash 1992; Rose 1985).

6. As explored in Chapters 4 and 6. The therapeutic value of research interviews has been noted by Etherington (2009).

7. Similar points have been made by Herman (2001), Dutton (1992) and Sanderson (2008), among many others.

8. There has been considerable debate as to whether it is necessary for services for women to be provided and run by women alone, and, increasingly, whether the provision of generic services (i.e. services catering for both men and women) should be considered. Those who argue for the provision of women for women services point out that equality of treatment does not necessarily promote equality of outcomes, since services structured around men as citizens may not meet the differing needs of women (Coleman and Guildford 2001; Corston 2007). A report by the Women's Resource Centre (2007) found that these services were both needed and wanted by women and resulted in significant and positive changes for service users.

9. Abrahams 2007; Kirkwood 1993; McGee 2000b.

10. Hague *et al.* 1996.

Chapter 9

Looking Forward, Looking Back

At the end of our last talk, Briony commented that it marked 'I think, probably, an end to the story really. It's like closing a book on that chapter of your life.' Women had left their abusive relationships, overcome practical and emotional difficulties, created new homes and built lives free from violence; now they were feeling more confident and looking into a future full of possibilities. Many of them were using the insights and understanding that they had gained from their experiences, both of abuse and of the process of recovery, to become socially active in helping others who were struggling with problems in their lives. And they also drew on this knowledge to send their own messages of support and encouragement to other women experiencing domestic violence and abuse.

Moving forward

Women had talked to me early on of their hopes and expectations for their new lives, once they had left the refuge. As their comments in Chapter 1 indicate, very few had specific plans; most aspirations were expressed in very simple terms – a new start, a new home, perhaps wider hopes for themselves and their children, in terms of personal success and achievement – while two had felt unable to look beyond the present moment. Now they had solid achievements to look back on and celebrate and, best of all, they felt they had a future to look forward to.

Lindy had been the woman with the most explicit plans for the future, including being strong enough to reject her abuser's pleas to return. She had completely forgotten her comments and was astonished to listen to them again. 'I've done it, haven't I? Oh wow!' was her reaction. Now professionally qualified and in full-time work, she had already started to think about what she wanted to do in the next five years:

I would like to be in a management position in a job. I've got the itch to succeed, I think. I don't want to be at the bottom of the pile any more.

Envisaging any future for themselves had, at one time, seemed impossible either to Briony or Gemma. Both had come a long way in the intervening years. Briony now knew that she and her children had a future and that the family was working together to overcome their problems:

I do see that we have got a future. You know it's not just there for that day. We've actually got a future now. So…so that's one thing we've overcome. We are trying to look more positive. As I say, the future's before us, but you know, basically, how far in debt we are. And I keep thinking, right, carry on paying what I'm paying now, that'll be done by then. Oh, and that one will be done by then as well. Oh, so will that. You know it's worked out that at the end of July we will be debt-free. So…and we ain't going down that route again.

Gemma was also looking ahead – despite her many personal problems, she now had ambitions to obtain a degree and turn her experiences and new understandings into a career that would benefit others:

I think I've…I've grown in my…I've just grown, I've just grown. And… you know, I don't think I could have done it any other way, this is me. And I don't do things in a nice straight pathway, I do things like, you know, nice and zig zags. But I wouldn't learn any other way. I have had to make my own mistakes…and it is going to make me a fantastic social worker. It's a damned shame that I've had to lose my kids and had to be on this side of the fence. But I tell you, I am going to be so much more qualified than any other fucker that goes along there, because I will know it from this side… I'm becoming all I can be. That's the best way to put it, I think. I am becoming all that I am capable of being.

Although Gemma now had a clear idea of what she wanted for the future, other women had found their progress halted by unforeseen difficulties. Molly had, in fact, 'turned her life around', as she had hoped, but her worsening heart problems had curtailed this and she was now hoping that specially adapted housing and support would provide fresh impetus. She was, however, aware that she might not live to see this. For Jeannie, the need to move to yet another refuge and her subsequent housing problems had put her plans for a job and a secure future on hold, but she was definitely not going to sink back:

Just plodding on really. Just getting on with it basically. Nothing major. Do you know what I mean? But I just feel...I feel positive about it. I've just spent too many years being depressed and being down. 'Oh, no one don't care about me.' I just can't do it any more, 'cos it's not going to get me anywhere.

Once she had been rehoused, ideally close to her temporary accommodation, she hoped to return to her original plans and gain qualifications, possibly in social work. In the much longer term, there was a possibility that she and her children would start a new life in another country.

As the women reviewed their present lives, there was a feeling of justifiable pride in their achievements and a deep satisfaction with how things were, but also recognition of how they had changed and an optimistic view of their futures. Sally, with a new home, partner and family, felt that this was, indeed, a new chapter in her life. 'I think we're starting to be able to get on with our life now, where before we just couldn't,' she said. Charmian was also looking to the future:

When I think what I went through and what I've got now, I think, 'Right, on to the future.' I've got a better life now than I've ever had. I've got my life back on track. I'm more stronger. I'm more confident in myself. I haven't got a job yet, but that's why I went to college.

Getting a job was also an important goal for Sylvia, but her greatest pleasure had been in becoming part of her family again:

My own home that...yeah that's done, you know what I mean, I can move on. I think making new friends...you know...making sure Daniel was happy and settled and centred again...remaking contact with my family on a more regular basis because, with all that going on, it started being birthdays and Christmas [only]. Now I see my mum every week. I see my sisters every week. I chat to my brother by email every couple of weeks. So putting all those things back in place that I lost as that world closed in, you know, kind of forcing it back out again and embracing all that again. So I think the only thing that I've not done how I'd like to do it, I would have liked to have gone back to work earlier.

Sometimes, women found that what they really valued now was something they had not expected. Maddy, who had wanted 'a nice home', had discovered that independence and freedom to do what she wanted, when she wanted to, after total control in her life, was, 'Good, really good. That I can do what I like. I can put my pyjamas on and go to bed when I like and what have you, lock the door.' And Keira had come to recognise that she no longer needed to seek refuge in her work:

> And everything that I wanted to achieve for myself has really happened. I've changed, and for the better really. I was very work-orientated, now I'm not. And I think that's been for the better.

Leanne was another who felt that she had gained all that she had wanted – and something more as well:

> 'Cos all I wanted was a fresh start and a new life where nobody knew me – and that's exactly what I got. I've got my life back – and I've got my little boy back as well.

Her hopes for the future were simple and touching – 'just to be as happy as we are now'.

Finally, Liz, who had 'always wanted to do things', had achieved to an extent that frightened her:

> And now when I look back, I just think, out of me and my sisters, I've got the most professional job than they have. I'm the only one that drives and owns my own brand new car. Um…everything in my house is paid for. Patrick is successful at his job and he's happy. Jody, she's just thriving and just can't wait to claw her way through the world – I'm having to hold her back. I just wanted to be content. And even though it's, like, took seven year, I feel as if I'm finally there where it's quite scary having nowt to worry about. Can you understand me? It's like I han't got no worries. And that is the scariest thing because I think summat's going to come along, it's got to come along, I've always had summat to worry about. And having somebody else to share…I don't have to hold him up, whereas I have everybody else. I'm actually getting some me time and he's there for me and it's…it's not me putting all the effort in. It's quite nice to have some head space to, kind of, where you think, 'Now I've got some space in my head, what am I going to use it to do?' – if that makes sense.

Looked at in terms of Maslow's concept of human needs, as explored in previous chapters, women had built on a foundation of safety to create their own space within a community and grown in confidence and self-esteem. Now they were moving to the phase that he saw as the ultimate objective of growth: self-actualisation – extending their capabilities still further, exploring new pathways for themselves and taking the risk of moving beyond their existing boundaries. One of the ways they expressed this development was in reaching out to offer support to others.

Reaching out to others

When I first interviewed these women, either in the refuge or soon afterwards, many of them talked in general terms of wanting to help others in some way, to 'give something back'. Both in the refuge and in the immediate period after rehousing, the main focus of their lives was their own emotional and practical needs and those of their children. Dealing with the grief over all they had lost, regaining a sense of personal worth and establishing a new home and way of life in their communities rebuilt the structure of their lives. Then, as they grew in confidence and inner strength, they began to look outwards, to the possibility of realising their earlier ideas of helping others. They now recognised that their experiences and the insights they had gained had value for others facing difficult personal situations, and the compassion they had learnt towards themselves had given them an empathy with, and understanding of, other vulnerable individuals.[1] Gemma struggled to explain how she felt:

> Because, yeah, I've had the hurt, but I don't believe if I would have...if I hadn't have had that hurt, unfortunately, that I'd have the compassion I have. And the love that I have. Because, unfortunately, getting caved out, if you like, hollowed out with pain, gives you a huge capacity to love. It doesn't...some people can't empathise enough to take that on board. But I guess I wouldn't have [it] any other way.

At the time we last met, ten of the women had been, or were, reaching out to help others in some way. They did not talk readily about what they were doing to help others or want to make a big deal out of this – sometimes it was only a throwaway remark they made that led to the revelation of the work they had been doing. Indeed, it was only through the chance comment of a support worker that I learnt of the dedicated work of one woman. As I asked further about this aspect of their lives, however, it became clear that it was important for them to take this action and that they saw it as a way to achieve for themselves, but also to contribute something to society, as Sylvia explained:

> Which is why I went into doing the volunteering, so that I felt like I was still achieving something. And, okay, I've not come anywhere from it, like, financially, where I can do better things, but it still feels like I'm giving something back, without it interrupting what Daniel needs from me, you know.

Sometimes, the groups that women chose to offer help to were directly related to specific aspects of their own experiences. Gemma, for example, was supporting those who, like herself, had problems with alcohol misuse. Sylvia, who had herself struggled with debt, was now working as a volunteer in debt counselling, with the prospect that this might well turn into a permanent job. Other women felt drawn to work with particularly vulnerable individuals: both Liz and Lindy were in full-time work within the community, helping men and women with mental health problems and children with physical impairments.

Support for others who were in, or had left, abusive relationships was, perhaps, the most obvious way for women to offer help.[2] Not only did this enable them to 'give something back', either to the group that had helped them or to a similar organisation, but it also, as discussed in Chapter 4, provided a way of being in touch with like-minded and supportive people. Liz had become a volunteer in her local refuge fairly soon after being rehoused. Keira had also volunteered locally and was now hoping to become a full-time support worker, while Maddy, despite chronic health problems, travelled a considerable distance every week to help out at coffee mornings and other events at her local refuge. Two others were taking steps in this direction: Jeannie, although still in temporary accommodation, considered that she was now sufficiently mentally robust to apply to become a volunteer, and Lindy was also thinking about offering her services.

Workers commented that this desire to help others, particularly other abused women, often became apparent as women began to recover from the abuse; it was an indication that support from the refuge was becoming less necessary and that women were progressing successfully towards fully independent living. Care was needed in taking this step, however, to ensure that they were emotionally ready to move into this area; sometimes, this particular route to helping others was too much, too soon. Charmian had started work as a volunteer in an advice centre for abused women soon after leaving the refuge, but had found it had been too early in her recovery for her to be undertaking this type of work:

> It got to the stage where…I stuck it out for about a year and a half, but it was getting to me too much, because I didn't think I was ready to deal with other people's problems and I was having some of my own. And what they were experiencing, it was bringing…I were getting flashbacks, and it just didn't do me any good. I wanted to help 'em, yet I didn't have the strength. So I just said, 'Look I'm going to quit it for now.' So we'll just wait and see. 'Cos if they're sat there telling me

all about it and crying their eyes out, I'm very timid and I…I can get upset over adverts on't telly. So I thought, well, this is no good for me, because I'm going to be…start crying in a minute. And it's not fair for them, if you're not going to be strong for them. So I felt it wasn't for me. Not at the time anyway.

Although she was currently taking a break to recover from this emotional distress, she was confident that she would be returning as soon as she could, to an area where she felt she had something to give to others.

Women varied considerably in the amount of help they were able to offer at any one time. Some were constrained by the need to deal with their own problems, as Gemma explained: 'I can only give a little bit because I've got my own situation to deal with.' For Molly, the limitations were those imposed by her health problems. Previously a volunteer at a local family centre, she was now too ill to work and take an active role, but the restrictions on her mobility had provided another avenue to helping: acting as a mentor to troubled adolescents on her estate, who knew that she would be there when they needed her.

Opportunities to offer information and advice could also be engineered through work contacts. Leanne, whose job brought her into contact with students and young people, made a point of talking to them about domestic violence and abuse, its effects and why it was important to understand. As previous chapters have shown, women were often wary about talking about their experiences because they were unsure of the reactions of others. Suddenly, it seemed, there was a point where this reticence disappeared when it was a case of enlightening others about the effects of domestic violence and abuse. Lindy felt strong enough to challenge the general lack of understanding of abuse and the existing stereotypes of abusers and abused women:

> People do…when you think of a woman in a refuge, or a safe house, or whatever, you imagine this picture of a rough-looking woman and falling to bits. 'And that's not you, Lindy.' I said, 'But you can't put a …' I says, 'Put a row of men, choose the one who's the domestic violence…the one who's hitting his wife – you can't pick them.' They come from everywhere. I actually bumped into some characters from the cricket club one night. You know how you chat while you're waiting. And there was always this one woman, she always says hello, so we were chatting and she said oh…I can't remember what she was on about, she just all of a sudden opened up about her husband was hitting her. And I says, 'You don't have to stay there.'

Other women also seemed able to take this line when appropriate, not pushing their issues, but no longer afraid to stand up and be counted. They drew on their own experiences to do this within their own lives and were also glad to find, by participating in this research, a way in which they could offer peer support to a wider audience.

Messages from a new life

I had been privileged to walk with women for a part of their journey. As we neared the end of our work together, I asked them what message they would like to give to other women who were experiencing domestic violence. Their messages, recorded here in full, ranged from practical advice on obtaining evidence, dealing with the perpetrator and the mechanics of leaving, to words of hope and encouragement about the new lives they had found.

Two women focused on finding the courage to leave and seek help:

> Get out. Just leave as soon as you can. I mean, just don't even pack a bag, just walk out the door and just keep walking till you find somebody that'll help you. And don't go back. (Leanne)

> Get out. And go for it, you know. There's help out there, so they've got to do it. They've got to see that gateway and just go for it. (Charmian)

Maddy also saw the need to leave as the prime focus, but, echoing Keira's thoughts in Chapter 1, she emphasised that women had to feel ready in themselves to take this step: 'Move out of the house and go in a refuge. But in your own time, when you're ready to move out.' Listening to your own feelings and being fully committed to leaving was also part of what Lindy had to say:

> I think when you first get that message in your head – 'I don't want this any more' – go! Because that message keeps coming back. It's not until it's…usually when it's too late and something really drastic happens, you do actually get up and leave. Listen to your intuition. 'Cos I do…I do feel guilty what I put my children through. Because you want the rose-tinted glasses, don't you? 'This is my family and this is normal' – but it's not. So I do feel the guilt that I left my children in that lifestyle too long. So, no. Get out if you can get out. The recognition to say, 'Hello, this is here.' You don't have to put up with it. 'Cos I probably…I think if I met somebody who…I'd probably go and pack their bag for them. I'd want to go and say, 'Come on, we can do this.' But until that

person's ready, they're not going anywhere. So I say, when you hear that message yourself…

Like Lindy, Sally wanted women to think about the effects on the children of witnessing or being involved in abuse, and the need to protect them by leaving. Additionally, she emphasised the importance of women breaking their silence and telling someone about what was happening, both for their own sakes and to prevent harm to others:

> Call the cops sooner than later. Because the sooner you do it, they could get evicted. The longer you leave [it], they don't get…you've got to say…it's hard to tell anybody, but tell somebody. If it's not the police, tell somebody, because…I was screwed up for it because I didn't tell nobody. My kids got it because I didn't tell nobody. I didn't get out of the relationship. I don't want to see other women and children go through what my children's done, what I've gone through. Because, my friend that got raped by him…I said, 'Have you told anyone?' 'No.' 'Go and tell somebody.' She said, 'Sally, can I ask you, is it true what he done to you? Is it true what you put in your divorce papers?' I said, 'Why do you think?' Because she asked me before it happened [about the violence] and he was, sort of, like, lingering outside. And then he did it to her and I felt guilty as anything – because I didn't tell her. But I was too scared, because he was stood in the background. So tell somebody. Don't let your children go through what my kids have gone through. That is the one thing that I really am upset about, is that I let my kids go through what they went through. 'Cos I didn't tell nobody, didn't get out. It was hard. And I know it'd be hard for other women to get out of the relationship. But if their husband works, get out of it when they're at work. Don't tell nobody…don't tell him that you're going. As soon as he's gone, pack your stuff, get out of there. Or pack as much as you can and get out of it.

Gemma was concerned that women should get justice from the legal system:

> Get witnesses. Never be left alone with him. Get dictaphones, get video cameras in your corner. That's the only way you'll keep your house, is have some way to record it as evidence and get them put away. Indisputable evidence – gather it…whatever it takes. That may be sad that the woman's voice isn't heard, but women's voice is not heard. Our word against theirs. And they often get so isolated… completely alone and have nobody or nothing. And um…I suppose, okay, to women who might be there with domestic violence and suffering domestic abuse – it's not you – you don't deserve it. Alcohol

– you're just ill, it's an illness. And, you know, trust what you know is right and what you know is wrong. Definitely.

Leaving, telling someone about the violence and obtaining help were all messages designed to encourage women to take action against the abusive situation. But women also voiced warnings not to repeat the cycle of leaving and returning:

Get out while you can. No, seriously. I would say get away from it, don't put up with it. You know, 'cos you can only be a punchbag for so long, you can only be put under domestic violence for so long. I was for years, through two marriages, two divorces. At the end of the day you could end up losing everything. I mean I lost my children through my husband. You could end up losing your children, you could end up losing everything. So I'd say get out while you can. And don't go back to them. And don't go back. DO NOT GO BACK. (Molly)

Get out...get out, get help. And I would advise anyone, just leave. Just leave, because it's just going to be a cycle. And it'll probably be all right for a little while, but it will just go back again, do you know what I mean? And obviously it depends on what level, but...abuse is abuse. If you know to yourself that something's not right and you're not happy and your children are unhappy, then you shouldn't be there, it's simple. You shouldn't be there. (Jeannie)

Stay away. Don't go back. Cut off everyone and everything that was around you at the time. And just try and make a new life. 'Cos it can be done. And once you've done it for a bit, it does become easier. Because if you're going into a place like a refuge and then end up going back to where you came from, I think you've wasted time and a lot of resources. Yeah, 'cos they're there to help you and to help you stay away. So...and I think you end up being a lot stronger if you do stay away. You have to stay away. 'Cos to go back, it's just starting that cycle all over again. You know, if you keep going back, you'll never get away. So you have to stay away. But, yeah, it's hard cutting everyone off, you cut your family off for a while, you know, you cut all your closest friends off, everything you've known, for however many years. But you have to do it, or else you'll end up becoming basically nothing. You'll have nothing to look forward to, no future, you know. No, you've got to stay away. For the long term. And, as I say, it can be done. It's got to be done. (Briony)

And three of the women focused on how life can be so much better after leaving:

Very simple – don't put up with it, get out. Yeah. There is another life after. You've just to believe it. (Keira)

Don't be a victim. Don't be a victim. As soon as you think that the bad has outweighed the good, make an effort to get strong and get out. Because it really isn't as bad as you ever think it's going to be. (Sylvia)

As much as they're feeling scared now – and it is a scary thought to actually take the leap – it does get better. That's not the only life there is for them…definitely. Just takes, you know, a big brave step. (Liz)

These messages come from women who, as their stories have shown, have endured severe and systematic physical, emotional and sexual abuse over many years, and who, at some point in their lives, took the difficult decision to leave the relationship and find someone to help them. Home Office research (Hester and Westmarland 2005) indicates that it is women like these, who have suffered high and continuing levels of abuse, who will, eventually, seek assistance with their problems. The knowledge gained from these twelve accounts can, therefore, offer valuable insights into the support women need as they journey from abuse towards recovery and reconstruction.

These insights can be used in a wide range of settings, both in refuges and within the community, to offer appropriate support to women who have experienced or are living with domestic violence and abuse. They emphasise the prime importance of safety and the need for women-only spaces with services that focus on their needs. They offer an understanding of the long-term effects of abuse and the complex problems that may emerge and that require an holistic approach to support-giving. They also show the importance of not 'giving up' on women who live with domestic violence and abuse. Leaving a relationship, often after many years, is not a simple, straightforward decision, but lengthy and often cyclical, and women need to feel that help will be available for them, and that they will not be rejected if they seek help on several occasions before finally making a choice as to what is best for them and their children.

A final thought

Perhaps, above all, the message that these women have to offer to others is that, with courage and determination, new and better lives, free from violence, can be built. Life after leaving had not been easy for any of these women, and years later the scars of their experiences were still there beneath the surface. Whatever their future held, they were facing it with courage and a clear understanding that it was better than living with domestic violence and abuse. As Sylvia put it, reflecting on the times we had met together:

> Be it years apart, it's still that journey from when you saw me when I was, like, very insecure, couldn't talk to anybody, was rubbish, to the person more like what I was before all this happened. Not all the way there, and if I'll ever get all the way there, who knows, but I will always strive to get there. I said to my mum, I said, I sometimes feel like a spring flower. She goes: 'Why?' I goes: "Cos the bulb sits in the earth so long closed in on itself and then suddenly Mr Sun comes out, Mr Showers comes down, and out he bursts with all his glory you know and says, "Hello, world, here I am."' You know. And I says…it is that real feeling of rebirth…and at 46 it's a bit old to be reborn!

Notes

1. Development of feelings of compassion and empathy following the experience of domestic violence and abuse has also been noted by Sanderson (2008).

2. Kirkwood (1993) suggested that there were three dimensions to a successful life after abuse: understanding and addressing one's own needs, asserting those needs in other relationships and taking action to assist abused women generally.

Appendix 1

About the Project

Background

Between 2000 and 2002, I carried out interviews with 23 women who had left an abusive relationship and gone into a refuge run by members of the Women's Aid Federation of England. The aim was to gain a better understanding of their practical and emotional support needs during their stay in the refuge and as they prepared to move into the community, in order to enhance service provision. At the same time, I talked to those responsible for providing services on the ground: managers, generalist and specialist workers, support staff and volunteers. These findings were reported to the refuges involved and have now been published (Abrahams 2007). Subsequently, I was part of a team carrying out a similar study on behalf of the Office of the Deputy Prime Minister (now the Department for Communities and Local Government). Here, the research remit extended beyond issues to do with domestic violence and abuse to cover other groups considered to be vulnerable – young people leaving care, ex-offenders, teenage parents, and those with drug, alcohol or mental health issues. In this later study, which took place during 2003–4, a total of 20 women who had experienced domestic violence and abuse were interviewed while in a refuge and again six months later. The refuges that collaborated in this project included those run directly by housing associations, those managed by Women's Aid on behalf of housing associations and refuges owned and run by Women's Aid groups. The full report and a separate report on good practice are available on the internet (Supporting People 2007).

Valuable information was obtained from both of these projects, but I felt that what was still missing was any longer-term view of the challenges women faced as they rebuilt their lives in the wider community. The last time work of this nature was carried out in the UK was in the 1980s, and over a much shorter timescale (Binney *et al.* 1981; Pahl 1985). Since then, massive social, legal and economic changes have taken place, which have affected all our lives. Domestic violence, once a hidden topic, is now the subject of government policy in many areas, and support services for individuals affected by abuse are more widely available.

Given all these changes, it seemed that a new longitudinal study had much to offer to both policy makers and service providers; listening to women's experiences over a period of years would provide information on both short- and longer-term support needs, help to identify any gaps in service provision and assist in the development of appropriate, targeted and cost-effective services. Building on the broad areas covered by the previous two studies and extending this into the continuing experiences of women and children in their new communities would offer a greater understanding of the pressures and difficulties involved and establish a cohesive and unique body of information to assist further research in this field. A research grant from The British Academy enabled me to take the first steps in implementing this project.

Theoretical approach

The research was conducted using an approach based on Participative Action Research (PAR, Reason 1994) and informed by feminist research practice (Kaspar 1994). Both approaches are concerned with creating an open and collaborative relationship with all those involved in the project, recognising that they are the experts in their own lives and seeking to produce knowledge that will be of practical use to all of those taking part in the research. Inherent in this approach is the need to balance the power relationship within the research – an issue of particular relevance in working with a group whose experience of power and control had, in the past, been detrimental to them.

Making contact

Informal contact had been maintained with the refuge groups and organisations that had participated in the previous studies, and I was aware that the majority of the women had been rehoused in the local area. The groups were enthusiastic about the proposed project and offered their support and assistance in designing and carrying out the research. A further positive factor was that many of the women who had talked to me during the course of the previous two studies had spontaneously indicated that they would welcome the chance to meet again a few years down the line, to talk about how they were getting on with the process of rebuilding their lives. Additionally, previous experience had shown that women were more likely to respond positively to an approach when they had already met the interviewer.

Although women had indicated that they would be happy to see me again, this could not be taken as an invitation to contact them direct; they might well have moved away, changed their minds, or be in a new, non-violent relationship where the partner was unaware of previous contacts. It was also possible that they had returned to the abusive partner or were in a new abusive relationship, so that further contact might put them and their children at risk. With the guidance and support of the workers at the refuges and safe houses, a full risk assessment was carried out on those women whose whereabouts were known, in order to ascertain who might safely be contacted; where there was considered to be any risk to the woman, no action was taken. In the event, initial contact by letter was considered safe with 22 women, of whom twelve responded positively (54.5%). Three of these responses came from the original project and nine from the later research. The majority had been out of the abusive relationship for more than five years; for two women, the gap was over seven years. By factoring in interviews with refuge support and outreach workers, firm information was available on a further eleven women: five from the group who were not directly contactable and six from those who chose not to respond. This information was often corroborated during interviews with the women, when we talked about whether they had stayed in contact with any former residents. There was also a fair amount of anecdotal evidence on the outcomes for other women, but this was not considered to be reliable enough for firm conclusions to be drawn.

Clearly, it is not possible to know why some women chose not to respond to the invitation, and a variety of reasons might be involved: they may have felt that they had not lived up to the hopes and expectations expressed in previous interviews and seen this as a 'failure'; they may have decided to close the door on the past and did not wish to be reminded of it; or they might have been in a new relationship and felt that talking to me might jeopardise this. Those who chose to respond stated categorically that the main reason for taking part was to share the experience they had gained in their new lives, in order to help other women suffering domestic violence and abuse, and to improve service provision. To do this, they were willing to explore the difficulties and problems they had encountered, as well as their achievements. An additional reason, given by a number of them, was the perceived need to raise public awareness of the longer-term effects of abuse. It is interesting to note, and a possible indicator as to why these women chose to respond, that ten out of the twelve were actively involved in offering help to others in some way.

Method

All those who responded were given full information about the purpose and aim of the project and gave written consent for their participation and the subsequent use of the material. Semi-structured interviews, lasting between one and two hours, were then carried out at a time and place to suit them. (Broad details of the topics covered are at Appendix 2.) The interviews were taped (with the consent of each woman) and were then fully transcribed. After each interview, women were invited to complete and return an anonymous feedback form, evaluating the interview and adding any further comments or thoughts.

Broad themes from all of this material, together with that from the previous interviews, were then identified and used to structure a detailed report for all the participating agencies and organisations. A formal report was compiled for The British Academy and an abstract of the research forwarded for their archives (The British Academy award no SG-41644).

Ethical considerations

The University of Bristol, through its ethical review system, is concerned with protecting the rights, dignity, health, safety and privacy of research participants, as well as the health, safety, rights and academic freedom of researchers and the university as a whole (University of Bristol 2009). Ethical approval for this project to proceed was given by the School for Policy Studies Ethics Committee. Research was also guided by the standards and references of the British Association for Counselling and Psychotherapy (Bond 2004), which stresses the need to protect the rights of participants and emphasises the importance of personal integrity and respect on the part of the researcher. These guidelines were particularly valuable, given the effects of domestic violence and abuse on mental well-being and the potential for harm that could arise from unconsidered research.

The aspects of ethical practice that I considered to be especially significant to the conduct of this research were the nature of informed consent and the duty of care towards participants. Informed consent needs to involve a clear understanding of the purpose of the research, the use that will be made of the material and the participant's right to privacy, safety and confidentiality. The initial contact with all potential interviewees was by letter, outlining the purpose of the research and the areas to be covered. A telephone number was included to enable any concerns to be dealt with in confidence. At the interview, we discussed again the purpose of the research and the use to be made of the material, together with the right to confidentiality and anonymity, to stop the interview, speak off the record and to have a copy of the tape or notes of the interview. This information was also supplied as a written record, which women signed to indicate they understood these matters and agreed to take part in the research. A copy of this was given to each participant. It was important that this preparatory period was not rushed and that there was time to ask about these or any other aspects of the research before the interview started. It was at this point that it was also necessary to discuss the possible revelation of information on which I would not feel able to maintain confidentiality. This could involve child protection issues or the possibility of self-harm/harm to others. I emphasised that I might need to take action in those circumstances, but that I would discuss this with the informant first. In the event, none of these issues arose.

It is doubtful if 'informed' consent can ever genuinely be given before an interview commences, since unforeseen issues may arise during the course of the interview, questions or responses may trigger unforeseen difficulties, and sensitive and possibly damaging information may be revealed, posing moral and ethical dilemmas for the researcher and stress and anxiety for the interviewee. Consent, then, must be seen as an ongoing process, constantly under review and renegotiation. This was certainly the case in this research; as can be seen throughout this book, women now felt able to discuss in more depth many of their experiences, both during the period of the abuse and subsequently, and I needed to check back with them on a number of occasions as to whether they wanted to continue, to speak off the record or to pause before continuing the interview.

The duty of care towards participants requires that the researcher acts with awareness and sensitivity towards them, both during the interview and afterwards (Bond 2004). Interviewees may inadvertently reveal information that they had not intended to divulge, and even giving the interview may result in an unexpected emotional impact either at the time or at a later date. At the end of each interview, I checked with the woman that there were no immediate difficulties and that she had details of local and national support systems, should she need them subsequently.

A duty of care applies also to the needs of the researcher. Stress and anxiety can be caused by the interview material, the dilemma of how to respond, and the pressure of constant ethical choices, particularly when being trusted with sensitive and potentially damaging information. Within my research group (Centre for Gender and Violence Research) there was a substantial body of experience in feminist ethical approaches and I was able to draw on peer support during this time.

As discussed earlier, safety considerations were a prime consideration when making initial contact with the women. Although they had now left the relationship, physical safety remained an important consideration, both for my informants and for me. This entailed a constant awareness of security considerations in making arrangements for and attending interviews, including checking in by telephone before and after each interview. Strict security measures were also applied to all the addresses, telephone numbers and interview material.

Finally, ethical research demands reciprocity – a need to give something back to those who participate in the research. Reciprocity was met at group level by the production of a detailed report and nationally by an end-of-grant report to The British Academy. Reciprocity for individual participants needed to be a far more immediate process, since they were taking time out of their lives to talk to me. I dealt with this by the informal discussions at the beginning and end of the interviews and by encouraging formal and informal feedback. Informal feedback showed that women felt valued and respected in the interviews, seeing themselves as powerful in having information and being able to share it to help other women. It was also important to them to be able to tell their stories to someone who gave the gift of time to listen to them and who would bear witness to their truth. Only one formal feedback form was received, in contrast to the previous studies. Although this response was extremely positive, the overall response rate confirmed my thoughts that women were now 'closing the door' on this part of their lives.

Formal reports to national and local groups form one strand of dissemination. However, as a researcher, I feel that there is an ethical responsibility to go beyond this and to ensure, with others, that the information and knowledge gained is placed in the public domain, although I cannot predict the uses to which it may then be put. In particular, there is a responsibility to make known the views of the only group of participants who are unlikely to take this action on their own behalf – the individual women who spoke to me about their experiences. It has been this responsibility that has resulted in this book, dedicated to them.

Participants

Below is a list of the women who took part in this research, the year when I first met them and their ages at that time, together with details of the children and young people who were then with them. As indicated previously, all the names have been changed to preserve anonymity and, for similar reasons, no details of location are given.

Name	Age	Year	Children and young people
Briony	36	2003	Two daughters 9 and 7, son 4
Charmian	41	2002	Son 3
Gemma	23	2003	Two daughters 4 and 3
Jeannie	34	2003	Two sons 10 and 18 months
Keira	49	2004	Daughter 13, son 12
Leanne	25	2002	Son 8
Lindy	35	2003	Daughter 11, son 7
Liz	31	2000	Son 13, daughter 9
Maddy	49	2004	Son 12, daughter 12
Molly	35	2003	Son 3
Sally	31	2003	Daughter 10, son 5
Sylvia	42	2003	Two daughters 21 and 18, son 5

Appendix 2

Precis of Topic Guide for Interviews

This precis is broadly representative of the areas explored during each interview. As women had already met me, a considerable amount of information on their backgrounds and circumstances was already known. Successive conversations added to this base, exploring changes that had taken place in the intervening period and checking back on problems, plans and thoughts that had been expressed previously. Any mention of drug or alcohol dependencies, or other forms of self-harm were followed through, and any changes in the household discussed. As indicated in Chapter 8, it was important to ensure that each interview gave women time to reflect on both recent and past events, often seeing these in a different perspective as the years went by. Although there were specific areas to be covered, women were also able to talk about what they felt was significant for them at that time in their lives; each set of interviews was, therefore, a continuing conversation and varied for each of the women in the study.

1. Housing

- How long have you been here?

- Was this where you moved immediately after you left the refuge?

- What sort of tenancy do you have?

- Would you have wanted to move back into your old home, with legal protection?

- How many people are in the household?

- How have your children settled in? (if mentioned in previous interviews)

2. Moving in

- Did you feel ready to move out of the refuge?

- How did you feel you were treated by the housing authority?

- Were you happy to move to this accommodation and area?

- What sort of condition was it in when you accepted the offer?

- Did you have support in moving and settling in when you left the refuge?

- Who was that from? How did that work? Was it helpful or not?

- Did you have help from anyone else in moving in?

- What is it like living in this house now?

- What is the neighbourhood like?

- Do you feel safe living here?

- What was the best thing about coming here?

- What were the difficulties? How did you overcome them?

3. Current formal support

- Have there ever been times when you have needed further support?

- Why was that? Whom did you approach?

- What did they do? Was that helpful?

4. Current informal support

- Where else do you get support from?

- Are you still in touch with any of the women you met while you were in the refuge(s)?

- How about the people round here?

- Do you feel a part of this community?

- Which are the most important contacts to you?

- Who would you turn to if you had a problem?

5. Work/education/leisure

- Are you in work, training or education at the moment?

- Are there difficulties that stop you working or joining a training scheme?

- Do you think you might take up work or training in the future?

- Are you hoping to get more qualifications?

- Do you take part in any other activities?

- Are you able to take the children on days out? Holidays?

- How are they getting on? Career plans?

- How about time for you?

6. Well-being

- How would you describe your physical health at the moment?

- How about your emotional health?

- Are you in contact with any health professionals?

- Are you involved with any other agencies?

- Did you continue/start counselling or groupwork after leaving the refuge?

7. Continued contact

- Do you have any continued contact with the person or people who abused you?

- How does that situation work out for you?

- (If appropriate) What is the legal position at the moment?

- Have there been any further problems – financial, further physical or emotional abuse etc.?

- Have you or your children been the victim of any crime or abuse since being here?

- What happened?

8. Overview

- What were your hopes and expectations on leaving the refuge?

- Have they been met? In what way?

- What have been your biggest successes? Problems?

- What are you proudest of?

- What is most important in your life at the moment?

- Compared with your life before the refuge, do you feel you are better or worse off now?

- Do you think your experiences since you left the relationship have changed you?

- Are there other changes that have affected your life since we met?

- How do you see yourself now as compared to when you were in the relationship?

- Are there any changes in the way you relate to people now?

- Looking back to the time you spent in the refuge, what do you remember most?

- What do you see as having been most useful? Problems?

- Has there been any lasting effect? Altered perspectives?

- Was there anything else you would have liked in the way of support?

  o   In the refuge? After you had left?

- Do you think that refuges should provide women-only services for women?

- How about official services – who should staff them?

- What do you look for in receiving services now?

9. Future

- Where do you see yourself in five years?

- What are your long-term aims, plans/hopes?

- If you were able to give a message to other women, what would it be?

Resource Materials

All website addresses checked November 2009.

Below is a selection of the groups and organisations within the UK and Republic of Ireland offering support and information to those who experience domestic violence and abuse. Similar organisations now exist in many countries across the world.

It is important to be cautious when accessing any of the websites from a computer that an abuser has access to. Many of the sites contain information on actions that can be taken to minimise the chance that access might be discovered.

24 Hour National Domestic Violence Helpline

0808 2000 247 (minicom available)

Run in partnership between Women's Aid and Refuge. Freephone service for support, advice, information and access to a range of other services, including safe houses and outreach. Callers can be signposted to many other sources of help to meet individual requirements.

Associated websites are:

www.refuge.org.uk/

www.womensaid.org.uk/

Advice, information and support to those experiencing domestic violence and abuse, together with links to local groups and other sources of support on a wide range of associated topics. Sister organisations to Women's Aid Federation of England in Northern Ireland, the Republic of Ireland, Scotland and Wales are listed below and offer similar services within their localities.

Black Association of Women Step Out (BAWSO)

24-hour helpline 0800 731 8147

www.bawso.org.uk

Offers specialist advice and support to black and minority ethnic women who have experienced, or are experiencing, domestic violence and abuse.

Chinese Information and Advice Centre (CIAC)
Telephone advice helpline 08453 131 868
www.ciac.co.uk
Offers information and support on family matters, domestic abuse and immigration.

Freedom Programme
www.freedomprogramme.co.uk
Offers a twelve-week programme giving information to help women understand issues around domestic violence and abuse, and gain the self-esteem and confidence to improve the quality of their lives. Available at many venues across the UK. Links via website, or use search facilities on internet.

Hidden Hurt
www.hiddenhurt.co.uk
A domestic abuse website, run by a survivor, with information and support.

Irish Women's Aid (Republic of Ireland)
1800 341 900
www.womensaid.ie

Jewish Women's Aid
0800 59 12 03
www.jwa.org.uk

Northern Ireland Women's Aid Federation
24-hour helpline 0800 917 1414
www.niwaf.org

Rape Crisis
See telephone directory for local numbers.
www.rapecrisis.org.uk
National organisation operating local centres for women who have experienced rape or sexual abuse.

Rape and Sexual Abuse Support Centre
National Freephone Helpline 0808 802 9999 (12.30–14.30 and 19.00–21.00, 365 days a year)
www.rasasc.org.uk
Provides help and support for female and male survivors, as well as non-abusing families, partners, friends and other agencies. Callers outside London looking for services in the local area will be referred to the nearest Rape Crisis Centre.

Scottish Women's Aid
24hour helpline 0800 027 1234
www.scottishwomensaid.org.uk

Southall Black Sisters
0208 571 0800
www.southallblacksisters.org.uk
Specialist advice and support for Asian and African-Caribbean women suffering violence and abuse.

Victim Support
0845 30 30 900 (see also telephone directory or website for local services)
www.victimsupport.org.uk
Service for the victims of crime and those who are acting as witnesses in court.

Welsh Women's Aid
24hour helpline 0808 8010 800
www.welshwomensaid.org

Services for lesbians, gay men, bi- or transgender people

Broken Rainbow
0845 260 4460
www.broken-rainbow.org.uk
Service for lesbian, gay men, bisexual or transgender people experiencing abuse.

Services for children and young people and their parents

Childline
0800 1111
www.childline.org.uk

Childline Ireland
1800 66 66 66
www.childline.ie
A weblink for children and young people to use. Confidential counselling service for children and young people.

Dads' Space
www.dads-space.com
Website and contact run by Respect (see opposite), offering advice and information for all fathers, with chat line and links to other sources of support.

NSPCC Child protection Helpline
0808 800 5000
www.nspcc.org.uk (with a weblink for children to use)
Advice and information on child protection issues and parenting-related areas.

ParentlinePlus
0808 800 2222
www.parentlineplus.org.uk
Support, advice and information advice for parents, step-parents, grandparents, friends and relatives on parenting issues.

The Hideout (link from Women's Aid for children and young people)
www.thehideout.org.uk

Services for men experiencing domestic violence
Amen Ireland
046 9023718
www.amen.ie
Confidential helpline, support services and information for male victims of domestic violence and their children.

Men's Advice Line (MALE)
0808 801 0327
www.mensadviceline.org.uk
Advice and information for men in heterosexual or same-sex relationships who are experiencing domestic violence by a current or former partner. Run by Respect (see below).

Services for male perpetrators of domestic violence
Freedom Programme
www.freedomprogramme.co.uk
Offers a training programme, giving information and helping men to change or improve their behaviour. Available at a number of venues across the UK. Links via website, or use search facilities on internet.

Respect
0845 122 8609
www.respect.uk.net
National association for those running perpetrator programmes and associated support schemes. Also runs the Men's Advice Line and Dads' Space (advice on parenting).

The Everyman Project
0207 263 8884
www.everymanproject.co.uk
Service providing advice, information, counselling and anger management services to men wishing to end abusive behaviour.

Services for elderly people

Action on Elder Abuse
0808 808 8141
Republic of Ireland 1800 940 010
www.elderabuse.org.uk
Confidential helpline providing information and emotional support to the elderly and their carers and to professionals on all aspects of elder abuse.

Bibliography

Abrahams, C. (1994) *The Hidden Victims: Children and Domestic Violence*. London: NCH Action for Children.

Abrahams, H. (2004) *A Long Hard Road To Go By: A Study of the Support Work Carried Out in Women's Aid Refuges*. Unpublished PhD thesis, University of Bristol.

Abrahams, H. (2007) *Supporting Women after Domestic Violence; Loss, Trauma and Recovery*. London: Jessica Kingsley Publishers.

Allnock, D. with Bunting, L., Price, A., Morgan-Klein, N. *et al.* (2009) *Sexual Abuse and Therapeutic Services for Children and Young People: The Gap Between Provision and Need*. London: NSPCC. Accessed on 20 October 2009 at www.nspcc.org.uk/inform/research/Findings/sexual_abuse_therapeutic_services_wda67007.html

Arnold, L. and Magill, A. (2000) *Making Sense of Self-Harm*. Abergavenny: The Basement Project.

Barns, R. with Abrahams, H. (2008) *Pilot Evaluation of Survive Services*. Bristol: University of Bristol in association with Survive, Kingswood.

Barron, J. (2004) *Struggle to Survive: Challenges for Delivering Services on Mental Health, Substance Misuse and Domestic Violence*. Bristol: Women's Aid Federation of England.

Batsleer, J., Burman, E., Chantler, K., McIntosh, H. *et al.* (2002) *Domestic Violence and Minoritisation: Supporting Women to Independence*. Manchester: Manchester Metropolitan University.

Binney, V., Harkell, G. and Nixon, J. (1981) *Leaving Violent Men*. Bristol: Women's Aid Federation of England.

Bond, T. (Second edition 2000) *Standards and Ethics for Counselling in Action*. London: Sage.

Bond, T. (2004) *Ethical Guidelines for Researching Counselling and Psychotherapy*. Rugby: BACP.

British Association for Counselling and Psychotherapy (2002) *Ethical Framework for Good Practice in Counselling and Psychotherapy*. Rugby: BACP.

CAADA (Co-ordinated Action against Domestic Abuse) (2009) *National Definition of IDVA Work*. Accessed on 22 October 2009 at www.caada.org.uk

Campbell, J., Rose, L., Kub, J. and Nedd, D. (1998) 'Voices of strength and resistance: A contextual and longitudinal analysis of women's responses to battering.' *Journal of Interpersonal Violence 13*, 6, 743–762.

Charles, N. (1994) 'The housing needs of women and children escaping domestic violence.' *Journal of Social Policy 23*, 4, 465–487.

Clifton, J. (1985) 'Refuges and Self-Help.' In N. Johnson (ed.) *Marital Violence.* London: Routledge and Kegan Paul.

Coleman, E. and Guildford, A. (2001) 'Threshold Women's Mental Health Initiative: Striving to keep women's mental health issues on the agenda.' *Feminist Review Summer 2001,* 68, 173–180.

Communities and Local Government (2009) *Decent Homes and Council Housing Finance.* London: Communities and Local Government. Accessed on 20 October 2009 at www.communities.gov.uk/housing/decenthomes/

Cooper, M. (2008) *Essential Research Findings in Counselling and Psychotherapy: The Facts are Friendly.* London: Sage.

CordisBright Consulting Ltd (2006) *Evaluation of the Freedom Programme Medway.* Unpublished report for the Children's Fund, Medway.

Corston, J. (2007) *The Corston Report: The Need for a Distinct, Radically Different, Visibly-Led, Strategic, Proportionate, Holistic, Woman-Centred, Integrated Approach.* London: Home Office.

Coy, M., Kelly, L. and Foord, J. (2009) *Map of Gaps 2: The Postcode Lottery of Violence Against Women Support Services in Britain.* End Violence against Women/Equality and Human Rights Commission. Accessed on 20 October 2009 at www.equalityhumanrights.com/uploaded_files/research/map_of_gaps2.pdf

Craven, P. (2000) *The Freedom Programme.* Accessed on 20 October 2009 at www.freedomprogramme.co.uk

Damant, D., Lapierre, S., Lebossé, C., Thibault. S. *et al.* (2009) 'Women's abuse of their children in the context of domestic violence: Reflection from women's accounts.' *Child and Family Social Work.* Early View published online September 2009. Accessed on 20 October 2009 at www3.interscience.wiley.com/journal/120735670/issue

Davis, C. (2003) *Housing Associations – Rehousing Women Leaving Domestic Violence: New Challenges and Good Practice.* Bristol: The Policy Press.

Deacon, A. (1995) 'Spending More to Achieve Less? Social Security Since 1945.' In D. Gladstone (ed.) *British Social Welfare: Past, Present and Future.* London: UCL Press.

Dimeff, L. and Lineham, M. (2001) 'Dialectical behaviour therapy in a nutshell'. *The California Psychologist 34*, 10–13. Accessed on 19 October 2009 at www.dbtselfhelp.com/DBTinanutshell.pdf

Dobash, R. and Dobash, R. (1979) *Violence Against Wives: A Case Against the Patriarchy.* New York: The Free Press.

Dobash, R. and Dobash, R. (1992) *Women, Violence and Social Change.* London: Routledge.

Dobash, R., Dobash, R., Cavanagh, K. and Lewis, R. (2000) *Changing Violent Men.* London: Sage.

Dutton, M. (1992) *Empowering and Healing the Battered Woman: A Model for Assessment and Intervention.* New York: Springer Publishing Co.

Etherington, K. (2009) 'Life story research: A relevant methodology for counsellors and psychotherapists.' In *Counselling and Psychotherapy Research*. Accessed on 20 October 2009 at www.informaworld.com/smpp/title-content=1713734893

Feder, G., Ramsay, J., Dunne, D., Rose, M. *et al.* (2009) *How Far Does Screening Women for Domestic (Partner) Violence in Different Health-Care Settings Meet Criteria for a Screening Programme? Systematic Reviews of Nine UK National Screening Committee Criteria.* NIHR Health Technology Assessment programme. Accessed 15 October 2009 at www. hta.ac.uk/1501

Government Equalities Unit (2008) *Women's Changing Lives: Priorities for the Ministers for Women One Year on Progress Report.* London: The Stationery Office.

Hague, G., Kelly, L., Malos, E., Mullender, A. with Debbonaire, T. (1996) *Children, Domestic Violence and Refuges: A Study of Needs and Responses.* Bristol: Women's Aid Federation of England.

Hague, G., Mullender, A., Aris, R. and Dear, W. (2002) *Abused Women's Perspectives: Responsiveness and Accountability of Domestic Violence and Inter-Agency Initiatives.* End of Award Report to ESRC, Award No. L133251017. Bristol: University of Bristol/ University of Warwick.

Heath, I. (2003) 'The Meaning of Domestic Violence.' In S. Amiel and I. Heath (eds) *Family Violence in Primary Care.* Oxford: Oxford University Press.

Herman, J. (Second edition 2001) *Trauma and Recovery.* London: Pandora.

Hester, M. and Pearson, C. (1998) *From Periphery to Centre: Domestic Violence in Work with Abused Children.* Bristol: The Policy Press.

Hester, M., Pearson, C., Harwin, N. with Abrahams, H. (Second edition 2007) *Making an Impact.* London: Jessica Kingsley Publishers.

Hester, M. with Scott, J. (2000) *Women in Abusive Relationships: Groupwork and Agency Support.* Sunderland: University of Sunderland.

Hester, M. and Westmarland, N. (2005) *Tackling Domestic Violence: Effective Interventions and Approaches.* Home Office Research Study No. 290. London: Home Office.

Hester, M., Westmarland, N., Pearce, J. and Williamson, E. (2008) *Early Evaluation of the Domestic Violence, Crime and Justice Act 2004.* Ministry of Justice Research Series 14/08. London: Ministry of Justice.

Hirsch, D. (2008) *Estimating the Costs of Child Poverty.* York: Joseph Rowntree Foundation.

Home Office (2009) *What is Domestic Violence?* Home Office mini-site. Accessed on 20 October 2009 at www.crimereduction.homeoffice.gov.uk/dv/dv01.htm

Hoff, L. (1990) *Battered Women as Survivors.* London: Routledge.

Humphreys, C. and Joseph, S. (2004) 'Domestic violence and the politics of trauma.' *Women's Studies International Forum 27*, 559–570.

Humphreys, C. and Thiara, R. (2002) *Routes to Safety.* Bristol: Women's Aid Federation of England.

Humphreys, C. and Thiara, R. (2003) 'Mental health and domestic violence: "I call it symptoms of abuse".' *British Journal of Social Work 33*, 209–226.

Itzin, C. (2006) *Tackling the Health and Mental Health Effects of Domestic and Sexual Violence and Abuse.* Joint Deptartment of Health and National Institute for Mental Health in England in partnership with the Home Office. London: Department of Health.

Jaffe, P., Wolfe, D. and Wilson, S. (1990) *Children of Battered Women.* Newbury Park, CA: Sage.

Jones, A., Pleace, N. and Quilgars, D. (2002) *Firm Foundations: An evaluation of the Shelter 'Homeless to Home' Service.* London: Shelter.

Joseph Rowntree Foundation (2009) *A Minimum Income Standard for Britain in 2009.* Compiled by a team from the Centre for Research in Social Policy at Loughborough University. York: Joseph Rowntree Foundation.

Kaspar, A. (1994) 'A feminist, qualitative methodology: A study of women with breast cancer.' *Qualitative Sociology 17,* 3, 263–281.

Kirkwood, C. (1993) *Leaving Abusive Partners.* London: Sage.

Lapierre, S. (2008) 'Mothering in the context of domestic violence: The pervasiveness of a deficit model of mothering.' *Child and Family Social Work 13,* 4, 454–463.

Lempert, L. (1996) 'Women's strategies for survival: Developing agency in abusive relationships.' *Journal of Family Violence 11,* 3, 269–289.

Livingston, M., Bailey, N., Kearns, A. (2008) *People's Attachment to Place: The Influence of Neighbourhood Deprivation.* Coventry: Chartered Institute of Housing in association with Joseph Rowntree Foundation.

Lodge, S., Goodwin, J. and Pearson, C. (2001) *Domestic Violence in Devon: A Mapping Exercise.* Exeter: Devon County Council and Devon and Cornwall Constabulary.

Lowe, P., Humphreys, C. and Williams, S. (2007) 'Night terrors: Women's experiences of (not) sleeping where there is domestic violence.' *Violence Against Women 13,* 6, 549–561.

Maslow, A. (Third edition 1987, first published 1954) *Motivation and Personality.* London: Harper and Row.

Malos, E. and Hague, G. (1993) *Domestic Violence and Housing: Local Authority Responses to Women and Children Escaping Violence in the Home.* Bristol: Women's Aid Federation, England/School of Applied Social Studies, University of Bristol.

Malos, E. and Hague, G. (1997) 'Women, housing, homelessness and domestic violence.' *Women's Studies International Forum 2,* 3, 397–409.

McCarry, M. (2009) 'Justifications and contradictions: Understanding young people's tolerance of domestic abuse.' *Men and Masculinities 11,* 3, 325–345.

McGee, C. (2000a) *Childhood Experiences of Domestic Violence.* London: Jessica Kingsley Publishers.

McGee, C. (2000b) 'Childhood Experiences of Domestic Violence.' In J. Hanmer, C. Itzin with S. Quaid and D. Wigglesworth (eds) *Home Truths about Domestic Violence.* London: Routledge.

McNaughton, C. (2005) *Crossing the Continuum: Understanding Routes out of Homelessness and Examining 'What Works'.* Glasgow: Simon Community.

McTiernan, A. and Taragon, S. (2004) *Evaluation of Pattern Changing Courses*. Exeter: Devon's ADVA Partnership. Accessed on 19 October 2009 at www.devon.gov. uk/pattern_changing.pdf

Mullender, A., Hague, G., Imam, U., Kelly, L., Malos, E. and Regan, L. (2002) *Children's Perspectives on Domestic Violence*. London: Sage.

Pahl, J. (1985) *Private Violence and Public Policy*. London: Routledge and Kegan Paul.

Parmar, A., Sampson, A. and Diamond, A. (2005) *Tackling Domestic Violence: Providing Advocacy and Support to Survivors of Domestic Violence*. Home Office Development and Practice Report 34. London: Home Office.

Penhale, B. (2003) 'Onward Referral to Social Services.' In S. Amiel and I. Heath (eds) *Family Violence in Primary Care*. Oxford: Oxford University Press.

Platt, His Honour Judge John (2008) 'The Domestic Violence, Crime and Victims Act 2004 part 1: Is it working?' *Family Law 38*, 642–647.

Povey, D. (ed.), Coleman, K., Kaiza, K., Hoare, J. and Jansson, K. (2008) *Homicide, Firearms Offences and Intimate Violence 2006/7*. Home Office Statistical Bulletin 03/08. London: Crown Copyright.

Povey, D. (ed.), Coleman, K., Kaiza, K., Hoare, J. and Roe, S. (2009) *Homicide, Firearms Offences and Intimate Violence 2007/8*. Home Office Statistical Bulletin 02/09. London: Crown Copyright.

Radford, L. and Hester, M. (2006) *Mothering Through Domestic Violence*. London: Jessica Kingsley Publishers.

Reason, P. (1994) 'Three Approaches to Participative Enquiry.' In N. Denzin and Y. Lincoln (eds) *Handbook of Qualitative Research*. London: Sage.

Robinson, A. (2007) 'Risk assessment and the importance of victim intuition.' *SAFE: The Domestic Abuse Quarterly 21*, 18–21.

Rose, H. (1985) 'Women's Refuges: Creating New Forms Of Welfare?' In C. Ungerson (ed.) *Women and Social Policy*. London: Macmillan.

Rothschild, B. (2000) *The Body Remembers: The Psychophysiology of Trauma and Trauma Treatment*. New York: W. Norton & Co.

Sanderson, C. (2008) *Counselling Survivors of Domestic Violence*. London: Jessica Kingsley Publishers.

Saunders, H. (2004) *Twenty-Nine Child Homicides: Lessons Still to Be Learnt on Domestic Violence and Child Protection*. Bristol: Women's Aid Federation of England.

Saunders, H. with Barron, J. (2003) *Failure to Protect? Domestic Violence and the Experiences of Abused Women in the Family Court*. Bristol: Women's Aid Federation of England.

Scottish Executive (2009) *Safer Lives – Changed Lives: A Shared Approach to Tackling Violence Against Women in Scotland*. Accessed on 20 October 2009 at www.scotland. gov.uk/publications

Siddiqui, M. (2003) 'Asian and Ethnic Minority Women's Groups.' In S. Amiel and I. Heath (eds) *Family Violence in Primary Care*. Oxford: Oxford University Press.

Stanley, N., Miller, P., Richardson Foster, H. and Thomson, G. (2009) *Children and Families Experiencing Domestic Violence: Police and Children's Social Services' Responses.* London: NSPCC. Accessed on 19 October 2009 at www.nspcc.org.uk/inform/research/Findings/children_experiencing_domestic_violence_wda68549.html

Stark, E. and Flitcraft, A. (1996) *Women at Risk: Domestic Violence and Women's Health.* London: Sage.

Stevens, M. and McDonald, R. (2000) 'Assessment of Women Who Seek Shelter from Abusing Partners.' In J. Vincent and R. Jouriles (eds) *Domestic Violence: Guidelines for Research-Informed Practice.* London: Jessica Kingsley Publishers.

Supporting People (2007) *Providing Housing and Support: An Evaluation of the Safer Communities Supported Housing Fund and the Approved Development Programme Pilots for Teenage Mothers.* London: Department for Communities and Local Government. Accessed on 20 October 2009 at www.spkweb.org.uk/Subjects/Supporting_People_independent_review/

Tischler, V., Edwards, V. and Vostanis, P. (2009) 'Working therapeutically with mothers who experience the trauma of homelessness: An opportunity for growth.' *Counselling and Psychotherapy Research 9*, 1, 42–46.

Turp, M. (2003) *Hidden Self-Harm: Narratives from Psychotherapy.* London: Jessica Kingsley Publishers.

University of Bristol (2009) *Research Ethics.* Accessed on 3 November 2009 at www.bristol.ac.uk/fssl/research/documents/researchethics.html

Walby, S. and Olsen, W. (2002) *The Impact of Women's Position in the Labour Market on Pay and Implications for UK Productivity: Report to the Women and Equality Unit.* London: Department for Trade and Industry.

Waldfogel, J. and Garnham, A. (2008) *Childcare and Child Poverty.* York: Joseph Rowntree Foundation.

Walker, L. (1993) 'The Battered Woman Syndrome is a Psychological Consequence of Abuse.' In R. Gelles and D. Loseke (eds) *Current Controversies on Family Violence.* London: Sage.

Williamson, E. (1999) 'Caught in Contradictions.' In J. Radford, M. Friedberg and L. Harne (eds) *Women, Violence and Strategies for Action.* Buckingham: Open University Press.

Women's Budget Group (2008) *Women and Poverty: Experiences, Empowerment and Engagement.* York: Joseph Rowntree Foundation.

Women's Resource Centre (2007) *Why Women Only? The Value and Benefits of By Women, For Women Services.* London: Women's Resource Centre.

Subject Index

204 / REBUILDING LIVES AFTER DOMESTIC VIOLENCE

Author Index

Quilgars, D. 46n

Radford, L. 143n, 144n, 161n
Reason, P. 176
Robinson, A. 30n
Rothschild, B. 123n

Sampson, A. 67n
Sanderson, C. 122n, 161n,
    162n, 174n
Saunders, H. 144n
Scottish Executive 19
Siddiqui, M. 122n
Stanley, N. 144n
Stark, E. 122n, 123n, 144n
Stevens, M. 122n
Supporting People 46n, 67n,
    144n, 161n, 175

Taragon, S. 85n
Thiara, R. 51, 67n, 85n, 103n,
    122n, 123n, 128, 144n,
    161n
Tischler, V. 161n
Turp, M. 122n

University of Bristol 178

Vostanis, P. 161n

Walby, S. 103n
Waldfogel, J. 103n
Walker, L. 123n
Westmarland, N. 67n, 80, 173
Williams, S. 30n
Williamson, E. 123n
Wilson, S. 144n
Wolfe, D. 144n
Women's Budget Group 103n,
    122n, 161n
Women's Resource Centre
    162n